GREAT FIGURES OF
MYTHOLOGY

GREAT FIGURES OF
MYTHOLOGY

PETER CLAYTON

with contributions by
Dr Irving Finkel   George Hart
additional material by
Alison Smart   Peter Thresh

INTRODUCTION BY
JOSEPH CAMPBELL

CRESCENT

Page 1   A drunken procession of
nymphs and satyrs escorts Silenus in
his cart as part of the Bacchanalia, feast
of the Roman wine god Bacchus. Not
even the horse is sober.

Page 2   The Greek god Heracles,
wielding his club, and Apollo, wearing
a wreath of bay as god of music, fight
for the tripod.

Page 4/5   The great theater at
Dodona, the oldest known sanctuary
of Zeus in Greece. Theatrical
performances originated in the ritual
ceremonies associated with religious
worship.

This 1990 edition published by Crescent Books
distributed by Outlet Book Company, Inc.
a Random House Company,
225 Park Avenue South
New York, NY 10003

Produced by
Brompton Books Corp
15 Sherwood Place
Greenwich, CT 06830

Printed in Hong Kong

ISBN 0-517-00538-7

h g f e d c b a

CONTENTS

INTRODUCTION
BY JOSEPH CAMPBELL
From *The Hero with a Thousand Faces*

Whether we listen with aloof amusement to the drama like mumbo jumbo of some red-eyed witch doctor of the Congo, or read with cultivated rapture thin translations from the sonnets of the mystic Lao-tse; now and again crack the hard nutshell of an argument of Aquinas, or catch suddenly the shining meaning of a bizarre Eskimo fairy tale: it will be always the one, shape-shifting yet marvelously constant story that we find, together with a challengingly persistent suggestion of more remaining to be experienced than will ever be known or told.

Throughout the inhabited world, in all times and under every circumstance, the myths of man have flourished; and they have been the living inspiration of whatever else may have appeared out of the activities of the human body and mind. It would not be too much to say that myth is the secret opening through which the inexhaustible energies of the cosmos pour into human cultural manifestation. Religions, philosophies, arts, the social forms of primitive and historic man, prime discoveries in science and technology, the very dreams that blister sleep, boil up from the basic, magic ring of myth.

The wonder is that the characteristic efficacy to touch and inspire deep creative centers dwells in the smallest nursery fairy tale – as the flavor of the ocean is contained in a droplet or the whole mystery of life within the egg of a flea. For the symbols of mythology are not manufactured; they cannot be ordered, invented, or permanently suppressed. They are spontaneous productions of the psyche, and each bears within it, undamaged, the germ power of its source.

What is the secret of the timeless vision? From what profundity of the mind does it derive? Why is mythology everywhere the same, beneath its varieties of costume? And what does it teach?

Today many sciences are contributing to the analysis of the riddle. Archaeologists are probing the ruins of Iraq, Honan, Crete, and Yucatan. Ethnologists are questioning the Ostiaks of the river Ob, the Boobies of Fernando Po. A generation of orientalists has recently thrown open to us the sacred writings of the East, as well as the pre-Hebrew sources of our own Holy Writ. And meanwhile another host of scholars, pressing researches begun last century in the field of folk psychology, has been seeking to establish the psychological bases of language, myth, religion, art development, and moral codes.

Most remarkable of all, however, are the revelations that have emerged from the mental clinic. The bold and truly epoch-making writings of the psychoanalysts are indispensable to the student of mythology; for, whatever may be thought of the detailed and sometimes contradictory interpretations of specific cases and problems, Freud, Jung, and their followers have demonstrated irrefutably that the logic, the heroes, and the deeds of myth survive into modern times. In the absence of an effective general mythology, each of us has his private, unrecognized, rudimentary, yet secretly potent pantheon of dream.

Far left The temple at Paestum in southern Italy dedicated to Athena, Greek goddess of wisdom. Paestum was a major cult center in the archaic period.

Below The Greek hero Achilles lies in wait behind a fountain for the Trojan Troilus, from a second century BC drinking vessel.

Right Sixth century BC bronze of Apollo, with characteristic archaic smile and patterned hair.

Right Pagan Celtic figures on Boa Island, Lough Erne, Ireland. These date from the fifth or sixth century AD but the style of worship they reflect dates back to well before the Christian era.

The unconscious sends all sorts of vapors, odd beings, terrors, and deluding images up into the mind – whether in dream, broad daylight or insanity; for the human kingdom, beneath the floor of the comparatively neat little dwelling that we call our consciousness, goes down into unsuspected Aladdin caves. There not only jewels but also dangerous jinn abide: the inconvenient or resisted psychological powers that we have not thought or dared to integrate into our lives. And they may remain unsuspected, or, on the other hand, some chance word, the smell of a landscape, the taste of a cup of tea, or the glance of an eye may touch a magic spring, and then dangerous messengers begin to appear in the brain. These are dangerous because they threaten the fabric of the security into which we have built ourselves and our family. But they are fiendishly fascinating too, for they carry keys that open the whole realm of the desired and feared adventure of the discovery of the self. Destruction of the world that we have built and in which we live, and of ourselves within it; but then a wonderful reconstruction, of the bolder, cleaner, more spacious, and fully human life – that is the lure, the promise and terror, of these disturbing night visitants from the mythological realm that we carry within.

Psychoanalysis, the modern science of reading dreams, has taught us to take heed of these unsub-

Left The Trojan Horse, a huge wooden model with which the Greek besiegers deceived the Trojans into letting them into the city; from an archaic Greek funerary urn.

Below Thoth, the Egyptian sun god, acting as a scribe on a relief from the temple of Rameses II at Luxor.

stantial images. Also it has found a way to let them do their work. The dangerous crises of self-development are permitted to come to pass under the protecting eye of an experienced initiate in the lore and language of dreams, who then enacts the role and character of the ancient mystagogue, or guide of souls, the initiating medicine man of the primitive forest sanctuaries of trial and initiation. The doctor is the modern master of the mythological realm, the knower of all the secret ways and words of potency. His role is precisely that of the Wise Old Man of the myths and fairy tales whose words assist the hero through the trials and terrors of the weird adventure. He is the one who appears and points to the magic shining sword that will kill the dragon-terror, tells of the waiting bride and the castle of many treasures, applies healing balm to the almost fatal wounds, and finally dismisses the conqueror, back into the world of normal life, following the great adventure into the enchanted night.

When we turn now, with this image in mind, to consider the numerous strange rituals that have been reported from the primitive tribes and great civilizations of the past, it becomes apparent that the purpose and actual effect of these was to conduct people across those difficult thresholds of transformation that demand a change in the patterns not only of conscious but also of unconscious life. The so-called rites of passage, which occupy such a prominent place in the life of a

Above Detail of a Celtic rider god, from the silver helmet of a Thraco-Getic chief, fourth century BC, found in a Romanian tomb and part of a ceremonial suit of armor.

Mother, but to cleave to her. And so, while husbands are worshiping at their boyhood shrines, being the lawyers, merchants, or masterminds their parents wanted them to be, their wives, even after fourteen years of marriage and two fine children produced and raised, are still on the search for love – which can come to them only from the centaurs, sileni, satyrs, and other concupiscent incubi of the rout of Pan, as in our popular, vanilla-frosted temples of the veneral goddess, under the make-up of the latest heroes of the screen. The psychoanalyst has to come along, at last, to assert again the tried wisdom of the older, forward-looking teachings of the masked medicine dancers and the witch-doctor-circumcisers; whereupon we find, as in the dream of the serpent bite, that the ageless initiation symbolism is produced spontaneously by the patient himself at the moment of the release. Apparently, there is something in these initiatory images so necessary to the psyche that if they are not supplied from without, through myth and ritual, they will have to be announced again, through dream, from within – lest our energies should remain locked in a banal, long-outmoded toy-room, at the bottom of the sea.

The story is told, for example, of the great Minos, king of the island-empire of Crete in the period of its commercial supremacy: how he hired the celebrated artist-craftsman Daedalus to invent and construct for him a labyrinth, in which to hide something of which the palace was at once ashamed and afraid. For there was a monster on the premises which had been born to Pasiphaë, the queen. Minos, the king, had been busy, it is said, with important wars to protect the trade routes; and meanwhile Pasiphaë had seduced a magnificent, snow-white, sea-born bull. It had been nothing worse, really, than what Minos' own mother had allowed to happen: Minos' mother was Europa, and it is well known that she was carried by a bull to Crete. The bull had been the god Zeus, and the honored son of that sacred union was Minos himself – now everywhere respected and gladly served. How then could Pasiphaë have known that the fruit of her own indiscretion would be a monster: this little son with human body but the head and tail of a bull?

Society has blamed the queen greatly; but the king was not unconscious of his own share of guilt. The bull in question had been sent by the god Poseidon, long ago, when Minos was contending with his brothers for the throne. Minos had asserted that the throne was his by divine right, and had prayed the god to send up a bull out of the sea, as a sign; and he had sealed the prayer with a vow to sacrifice the animal immediately, as an offering and symbol of service. The bull had appeared, and Minos took the throne; but when he beheld the majesty of the beast that had been sent and thought what an advantage it would be to possess such a speci-

primitive society (ceremonials of birth, naming, puberty, marriage, burial, etc), are distinguished by formal, and usually very severe, exercises of severance, whereby the mind is radically cut away from the attitudes, attachments, and life patterns of the stage being left behind. Then follows an interval of more or less extended retirement, during which are enacted rituals designed to introduce the life adventurer to the forms and proper feelings of his new estate, so that when, at last, the time has ripened for the return to the normal world, the initiate will be as good as reborn.

It has always been the prime function of mythology and rite to supply the symbols that carry the human spirit forward, in counteraction to those other constant human fantasies that tend to tie it back. In fact, it may well be that the very high incidence of neuroticism among ourselves follows from the decline among us of such effective spiritual aid. We remain fixated to the unexorcised images of our infancy, and hence disinclined to the necessary passages of our adulthood. In the United States there is even a pathos of inverted emphasis: the goal is not to grow old, but to remain young; not to mature away from men, he determined to risk a merchant's substitution – of which he supposed the god would take no great account. Offering on Poseidon's altar the finest white bull that he owned, he added the other to his herd.

The Cretan empire had greatly prospered under the sensible jurisdiction of this celebrated lawgiver and model of public virtue. Knossos, the capital city, became the luzurious, elegant center of the leading commercial power of the civilized world. The Cretan fleets went out to every isle and harbor of the Mediterranean; Cretan ware was prized in Babylonia and Egypt. But at home, the queen had been inspired by Poseidon with an ungovernable passion for the bull. And she had prevailed upon her husband's artist-craftsman, the peerless Daedalus, to frame for her a wooden cow that would deceive the bull – into which she eagerly entered; and the bull was deceived. She bore her monster, which, in due time, began to become a danger. And so Daedalus again was summoned, this time by the king, to construct a tremendous labyrinthine enclosure, with blind passages, in which to hide the thing away. So deceptive was the invention, that Daedalus himself, when he had finished it, was scarcely able to find his way back to the entrance. Therein the Minotaur was settled: and he was fed, thereafter, on groups of living youths and maidens, carried as tribute from the conquered nations within the Cretan domain.

Thus according to the ancient legend, the primary fault was not the queen's, but the king's; and he could not really blame her, for he knew what he had done. He had converted a public event to personal gain, whereas the whole sense of his investiture as king had been that he was no longer a mere private person. The return of the bull should have symbolized his absolutely selfless submission to the functions of his role. The retaining of it represented, on the other hand, an impulse to egocentric self-aggrandizement. And so the king 'by the grace of God' became the dangerous tyrant Holdfast – out for himself. Just as the traditional rites of passage used to teach the individual to die to the past and be reborn to the future, so the great ceremonials of investiture divested him of his private character and clothed him in the mantle of his vocation. Such was the ideal, whether the man was a craftsman or a king. By the sacrilege of the refusal of the rite, however, the individual cut himself as a unit off from the larger unit of the whole community: and so the One was broken into the many, and these then battled each other – each out for himself – and could be governed only by force.

The figure of the tyrant-monster is known to the mythologies, folk traditions, legends, and even nightmares, of the world; and his characteristics are everywhere essentially the same. He is the hoarder of the general benefit. He is the monster avid for the greedy rights of 'my and mine'. The havoc wrought by him is described in mythology and fairy tale as being universal throughout his domain. This may be no more than his household, his own tortured psyche, or the lives that he blights with the touch of his friendship and assistance; or it may amount to the extent of his civilization. The inflated ego of the tyrant is a curse to himself and his world – no matter how his affairs may seem to prosper. Self-terrorized, fear-haunted, alert at every hand to meet and battle

Below The Greek hero Peleus and the warrior maiden Atalanta together attack the Calydonian boar, from a sixth century BC black-figure vase.

back the anticipated aggressions of his environment, which are primarily the reflections of the uncontrollable impulses to acquisition within himself, the giant of self-achieved independence is the world's messenger of disaster, even though, in his mind, he may entertain himself with humane intentions. Wherever he sets his hand there is a cry (if not from the housetops, then – more miserably – within every heart): a cry for the redeeming hero, the carrier of the shining blade, whose blow, whose touch, whose existence, will liberate the land.

The hero is the man of self-achieved submission. But submission to what? That precisely is the riddle that today we have to ask ourselves and that it is everywhere the primary virtue and historic deed of the hero to have solved. Schism in the soul, schism in the body social, will not be resolved by any scheme of return to the good old days (archaism), or by programs guaranteed to render an ideal projected future (futurism), or even by the most realistic, hardheaded work to weld together again the deteriorating elements. Only birth can conquer death – the birth, not of the old thing again, but of something new. Within the soul, within the body social, there must be – if we are to experience long survival – a continuous

'recurrence of birth' (*palingenesia*) to nullify the unremitting recurrences of death. For it is by means of our own victories, if we are not regenerated, that the work of Nemesis is wrought: doom breaks from the shell of our very virtue. Peace then is a snare; war is a snare; change is a snare; permanence a snare. When our day is come for the victory of death, death closes in; there is nothing we can do, except be crucified – and resurrected; dismembered totally, and then reborn.

The hero, therefore, is the man or woman who has been able to battle past his personal and local historical limitations to the generally valid, normally human forms. Such a one's visions, ideas, and inspirations come pristine from the primary springs of human life and thought. Hence they are eloquent, not of the present, disintegrating society and psyche, but of the unquenched source through which society is reborn. The hero has died as a modern man; but as eternal man – perfected, unspecific, universal man – he has been reborn. His second solemn task and deed therefore (as all the mythologies of mankind indicate) is to return then to us, transfigured, and teach the lesson he has learned of life renewed.

Far left Head of the glorious statue known as the Charioteer, one of the marvels of classical Greek sculpture, found at Delphi and probably dedicated to Apollo.

Above The cult of the all-embracing all-fertile mother goddess, which dates from the very earliest times, is here shown in restrained Roman style on the Altar of Peace dedicated by the Emperor Augustus in Rome in 13 BC. The earth goddess Tellus is surrounded by her offspring and by the flora and fauna of the earth.

ACHILLES

Perhaps the greatest figure in Greek mythology. It is around him that HOMER's the *Iliad* is woven: the tale of the wrath of Achilles as played out on the stage of the fall of Troy. His father was Peleus, king of Phthia in Thessaly, and his mother was Thetis, daughter of Oceanus (it is probably the story of their courtship that is told on the famous Portland Vase in the British Museum). While still an infant, his mother plunged him into the river Styx that divided earth and Hades to ensure that he would be invulnerable to any weapon. In so doing, however, she retained hold of him by his heel, and that was to be his downfall and the origin of the modern phrase for a person's weak spot, their 'Achilles heel'.

Thetis knew that Achilles would fall at Troy – he had the option of a short but glorious life if he went, or of a long inglorious existence if he did not. He was educated first by the centaur CHIRON and then Thetis tried to alter his fate by sending him away to the court of King Lycomedes, where he was disguised in female dress among the king's daughters. Wily ODYSSEUS, knowing it was prophesied that Troy could not be taken without the help of Achilles, went in search of him. Gaining access to the women's quarters disguised as a pedlar, he displayed his wares, having cunningly concealed fine weapons and a war

Far left Achilles on a fifth century BC vase.

Above Achilles and Ajax playing dice.

Left Priam supplicating Achilles for the body of Hector.

15

trumpet among them. When Odysseus sounded the trumpet, Achilles immediately seized upon the weapons, betrayed himself, and went off to the war with Odysseus.

To safeguard her son, Thetis persuaded HEPHAESTUS, the smith god, to make Achilles a fine suit of armor which was proof against any weapons. In a division of spoils during the war, Achilles lost his favorite mistress Briseis to AGA-MEMNON and then refused to fight; instead he sat in his tent and sulked. With Achilles absent from the fray the Trojans began to gain the upper hand, so Achilles' close friend, PATROCLUS, donned the armor of Achilles and went out to rally the Greeks but was killed by the Trojan prince, HECTOR, son of King PRIAM. This spurred Achilles to revenge and he killed Hector in single combat and then treated the corpse shamefully by dragging it around the walls of Troy behind his chariot. The gods condemned this treatment of the dead and forced Achilles to receive Priam, the grieving father, and restore the body to him for proper burial.

In the tenth and last year of the siege, PARIS, another of Priam's sons, found Achilles in the temple of Athena courting Polyxena, his sister.

Paris aimed an arrow at Achilles' heel, from which wound he died. There are countless stories of the deeds of Achilles in the *Iliad* and many others were invented and attributed to his name.

ACTEON

A hunter and grandson of APOLLO in Greek mythology who had been raised and taught to hunt by CHIRON the centaur. One day while out with his hounds, Acteon chanced upon the virgin huntress goddess ARTEMIS bathing naked in a pool accompanied by her maidens. Incensed by this intrusion, she changed Acteon into a stag and set his own pack of hounds on him; they failed to recognize him and hunted him to his death. His discovery of the goddess and his dreadful end was a favorite subject for vase paintings in antiquity and of painters in later centuries.

Right The great eight-sided Achilles dish from the Kaiseraugst treasure, Switzerland, shows episodes from the hero's early life and his education by the centaur Chiron, culminating in his discovery among the daughters of Lycomedes in the central roundel.

Above left   This early fifth century BC limestone relief from the Greek temple at Selinunte, Sicily, shows Artemis directing Acteon's hounds to attack the hunter, who is shown in human rather than stag form.

Above right   The artist who painted this early sixteenth century Italian dish represented Artemis changing Acteon into a stag against an idealized High Renaissance background.

Left   A human supplicant before the Mesopotamian weather god Adad and the goddess Ishtar, from an eighth century BC Neo-Assyrian relief.

ADAD

Mesopotamian weather god, son of An (also sometimes of Nanna-Su'en). Portrayed in mythological and religious texts both as a bull and a lion, Adad embodies the violent thundering rainstorms which sweep over the landscape of the Near East. In human form he is a warrior, riding his chariot harnessed to the storms across the sky. A common epithet for Adad is 'canal inspector of Heaven and Earth,' and he is involved with his brother SHAMASH in the administration of oracles. Adad had a temple in the city of Enegi near Ur, and in Babylon, and also a temple shared with his father An in Assur, the capital of Assyria. His symbol is a forked lightning bolt.

Right This mid-sixteenth century Italian plate from Urbino shows the unfortunate Myrrah being changed into a tree at the very moment of Adonis's birth. A group of lusty and wholly contemporary Italian peasant women act as midwives.

ADAPA

One of the Seven Sages of Mesopotamian mythology, and the hero of Akkadian myth which shares with the *Epic of Gilamesh* the theme of man's failure to achieve immortality. Adapa, a son of the god EA, lived in the city of Eridu, where he carried out cultic duties. While fishing in his boat one day he was suddenly wrecked by the South Wind. In return Adapa broke the wing of the South Wind by means of a powerful spell. Anu, chief god of the pantheon, despatched his vizier Ilabrat to summon Adapa to Heaven to explain the absence of this wind. Ea, wishing to save Adapa's life, recommended that he don mourning garb to flatter the two gods who man the gate, and told him what to say. Above all he was to reject any offered hospitality. Through following Ea's advice Adapa safely negotiated the gate and Anu's questions and was later released to return to earth, where his city received special favors but by having refused food and drink at Anu's hand he lost his chance of eternal life.

ADONIS

Although best known from Greek legend, the roots of his myth are firmly based in the ancient Near East around Syria and the Lebanon, where there was a river named after him whose waters were reputed to run blood red on the anniversary of his death. He was the son of Cinyras, King of Cyprus, himself a son of APOLLO. Adonis' mother was Myrrah, who developed an unnatural passion for her father Cinyras and tricked him into an incestuous union. When he discovered the deception he attempted to kill her but she fled to Arabia where, having given birth to Adonis, she was changed into a myrrh tree, giving it her name. APHRODITE loved the beautiful baby boy and gave him to PERSEPHONE to look after. Both goddesses were fond of him, especially Aphrodite as he grew into a handsome youth and she warned her lover against his passion for hunting. He was eventually gored to death by a wild boar and the goddess's tears (in some versions Adonis' blood) dropped to the earth and produced the blue anemone flower. Other legends say that Aphrodite changed him into the flower after his death.

See also ATIS, BALDER, OSIRIS, TAMMUZ.

AEGIR

The Norse god of the sea whose wife was the goddess Ran. He was the counterpart of the Greek POSEIDON, although the Norse god was far more frightening and had a darker side. The late fifth-century Christian writer Apollinaris Sidonius wrote that the Saxon pirates reveled in storms that would confound their enemies and, on their successful homeward journey, they would cast lots among their captives and consign every tenth one to a watery grave as a thank-offering to the Norse god of the sea.

Aegir is also noted as a giant who had nine daughters, identified with the waves of the sea, and his connection with earthquakes and storms is a further link with Poseidon. In another reference he is called 'the Ale-brewer' since he became the owner of a vast bronze cauldron in which he made the brew for the gods. The cauldron had been stolen from the giant Hymir by THOR and TYR (whose mother was Hymir's wife). Having been entertained by Hymir, Aegir challenged the two gods to lift the cauldron; Tyr failed but Thor put it over his head, its handles dangling around his ears, and ran off with it. A crowd of giants pursued them but Thor, placing the cauldron on the ground, proceeded to kill them all with his hammer.

Left The sea played a major role in Norse mythology long before the Vikings began their incursions. This savage wooden animal head, found in the Scheldt estuary, Belgium, probably ornamented the stern of a pre-Viking raiding ship.

AENEAS

A Trojan prince, the son of Anchises by the goddess APHRODITE or Venus. The most valiant of the Trojan heroes at the seige of Troy, he was to be found where the fighting was thickest and on several occasions was spirited away by various of the gods when he appeared hard pressed, because they were mindful of a prophecy that said he would rule the Trojans and his sons continue as rulers. At the fall of Troy Aeneas carried his aged father away on his back through the flames, together with his wife Creusa and son Ascanius. The scene was a favorite one for vase painters and also appeared on the coins of Julius Caesar (who claimed the Julian line to be descended from Venus via Aeneas). Subsequently, he embarked on widespread travels, arriving in Sicily where Anchises died and was buried. An adverse wind then blew Aeneas' ship to Carthage, where he was loved by DIDO, its queen, who wished to marry him. This sojourn forms a major element in the Roman poetry relating to Aeneas, especially that of Virgil where he is the protago-

nist of the great poem, the *Aeneid*. This was essentially a piece of propaganda for the Roman emperors' descent from the gods. Episodes from the *Aeneid* are common in Roman art, on all sorts of pottery and silver vessels, in painting, sculpture and on mosaics.

Aeneas, leaving Dido and Carthage behind, eventually landed at the mouth of the Tiber (having first visited the famous Sibyl at Cumae, who showed him Hell). He was hospitably received by the local king, Latinus, and after several battles with rivals and enemies married Latinus' daughter Lavinia (after whom the town of Lavinium is named), and succeeded Latinus as king. According to Roman tradition, Aeneas was drowned in the river Numicus in a battle against the Etruscans. His body was never found (probably due to the weight of his armor), but it was thought that he had been taken up by the gods and he was duly offered sacrifices as one of their number. Tradition also gives him four sons, Ascanius, Euryleon, ROMULUS and REMUS, the third of whom was the eponymous founder of Rome. Thus Virgil, and the Latin poets who followed him, could produce a lineage for the Roman emperors stretching back into prehistoric time and a relationship with the gods.

Right This wall painting from the Roman city of Pompeii illustrates the scene in Virgil's *Aeneid* where the doctor Iapis uses forceps to treat an arrow wound in Aeneas's leg. Aeneas leans on his young son Ascanius, while Aphrodite hovers protectively.

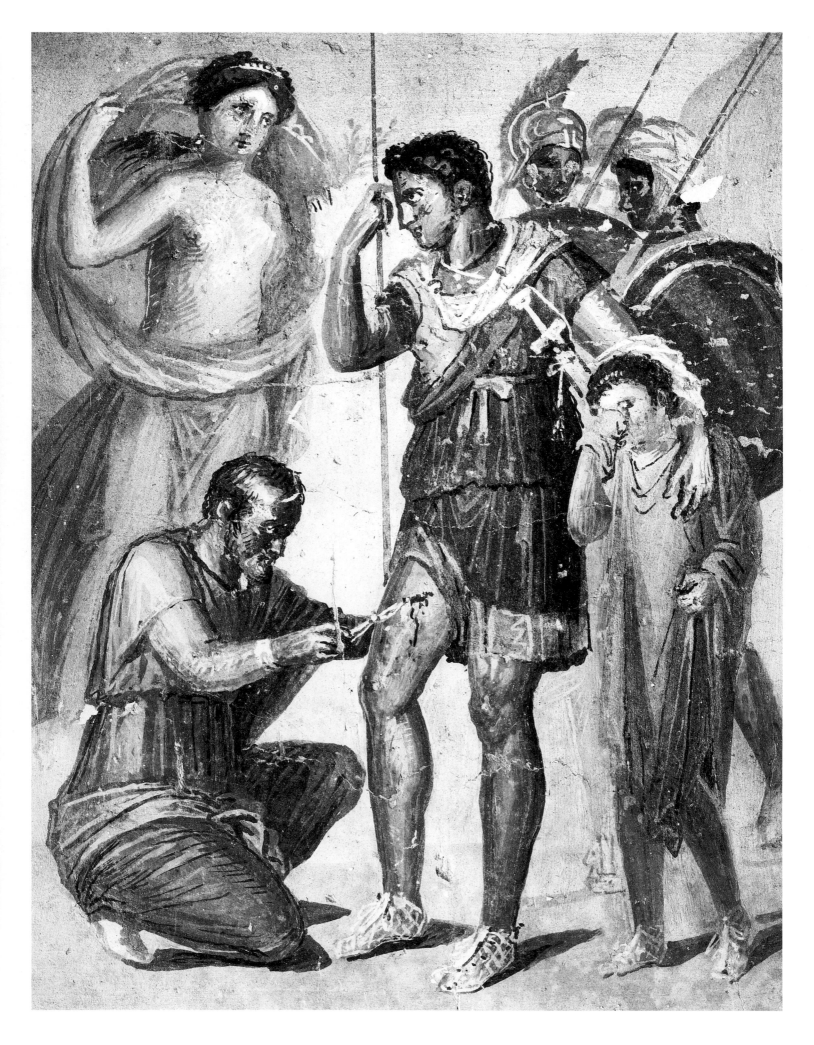

Right This gold death mask of an Achaean king was hailed by the archaeologist Heinrich Schliemann as the Mask of Agamemnon when it was found in the acropolis at Mycenae.

AGAMEMNON

In Greek legend, king of Mycenae and of Argos. His brother was MENELAUS, king of Sparta. The brothers married two sisters the daughters of LEDA by ZEUS, CLYTEMNESTRA and HELEN. Clytemnestra had previously been married to Tantalus, but Agamemnon killed both her husband and their infant son and then married her. Her brothers, the DIOSCURI, vowed vengeance but eventually agreed to make peace. The marriage was cursed from the start, however, as later events were to show.

At the start of the Trojan War, which arose because PARIS had stolen Helen from Menelaus, Agamemnon was elected as the leader of the Greeks, the Achaeans. On the way to Troy, at Aulis, in order to obtain a favorable wind, he sacrificed his daughter IPHIGENIA to Artemis. Throughout the Trojan War Agamemnon showed great bravery but a blight hung over the campaign because of his quarrels with ACHILLES, especially when he insisted on taking Achilles' mistress/ slave Briseis, as part of his due. The 'Anger of Achilles' in the ninth year of the siege was, in effect, the main theme of the *Iliad*.

After Troy had fallen by the subterfuge of using a hollow horse (the Trojan Horse) to introduce armed men into the city to open the gates to the Greeks, Agamemnon received CASSANDRA, daughter of PRIAM and Hecuba, as part of his spoils. Cassandra prophesied that Agamemnon would be killed by his wife, but he chose to disregard her. At home in Mycenae, however, Agamemnon's wife Clytemnestra had taken a lover, Aegisthus, and together they planned his murder. Accounts vary as to how the deed was committed but the most popular has it that when Agamemnon emerged from a bath Clytemnestra handed him a shirt with its sleeves sewn up. As he struggled to put it on she and her lover attacked him with axes and cut him down, also murdering Cassandra. The murder was a popular scene represented on Greek vase paintings. Agamenon's son by Clytemnestra, ORESTES, avenged his father by killing the murderers, with the consequent charge of matricide being leveled against him. See also ATREUS.

AHURA-MAZDA

Later called Ormuzd and principal deity in Zoroastrianism, the religion of ancient Iran. This doctrine, propounded by Zarathustra (Zoroaster), traditionally dated to 628-551 BC, entails a dualistic system of Good, created by Ahuramazda, opposed to Evil, embodied in Ahriman. Fire was central to Zoroastrianism, as is evident from excavations of Sassanian fire temples and the recurrence of fire altars on Sassanian coins. It appears that the Achaemenid kings (the dynasty founded by Cyrus, 550-530 BC), may well have been Zoroastrians, since such rulers as Darius, Xerxes and Cyrus describe Ahuramazda as the 'greatest of the gods' in their inscriptions, although without denying the power of other gods who find no mention in the Avestan literature. Ahuramazda is often considered to be represented in the characteristic winged disc containing a human figure found in Achaemenid sculpture, a device that itself derives from Assyrian representations of the national god Assur. Clear representations of Ahuramazda are found in scenes showing the investiture of the Sassanian kings.

AJAX

There are two heroes named Ajax in the Greek legends. To differentiate them they are often referred to as the Great and the Lesser Ajax; both served in the Trojan War but the former was the greater and more pleasant character.

Ajax the Lesser ws the son of Oileus, king of Locris. He was unpleasant in his manners and irreligious in his attitudes. The night Troy fell he pursued CASSANDRA to where she had taken sanctuary in the temple of ATHENA, clasping the cult statue. Ajax carried both her and the statue off and then raped the girl. Athena sought revenge for this impiety and destroyed his ship on the way home, but Ajax swam to a rock and boasted that he was safe despite the gods. This was too much for them and particularly for POSEIDON, who smashed with his trident the rock to which Ajax clung and he was drowned. His impiety lived on after him when epidemics broke out in Locris and there were bad harvests. An oracle said that these misfortunes were the result of Athena's continuing anger at the rape of Cassandra and violation of her sanctuary. The Locrians were then told to send a pair of girls, chosen by lot, to Troy each year for a thousand years. This was done; the first two were killed by the Trojans but subsequent

Left Detail from a Greek black-figure vase showing the two warriors Ajax and Achilles playing dice during a lull in the ten-year Trojan War.

Right One of the best preserved and most dramatic of all Greek black-figure vases shows Achilles, terrifying in his battle helmet, defeating and killing the Amazon queen Penthesilea. The legend was that he fell in love with her even as his sword pierced her breast.

victims, if they could escape the mob, spent the rest of their days, unmarried, in Athena's sanctuary.

Ajax the Greater was the son of Telamon, king of Salamis. After ACHILLES, he was the bravest of the Greeks. Totally different from the Lesser Ajax, he was noted for his courtesy, piety and good character. Several times he fought against HECTOR, but the gods had decreed that Hector would only fall to Achilles and so each time that Hector began to be worsted the gods rescued him. Ajax was noted for having taken numerous of the towns on the coast of Asia Minor.

At the fall of Troy Ajax suffered a series of setbacks. He demanded that HELEN be put to death for her adultery, but the brothers AGAMEMNON and MENELAUS were incensed at this and ODYSSEUS secured her return to Menelaus. Next, Ajax

demanded the Palladium as his share of the spoils. This was the statue of Pallas upon which Troy's preservation depended and which Odysseus and DIOMEDES had stolen. Once again he was thwarted by Agamemnon and Menelaus, who had to surround themselves with armed guards for protection against him. Another account tells how Ajax coveted the arms of Achilles which, after his death, were to go to the Greek who had most frightened the Trojans. A poll was conducted amongst the Trojan prisoners and they, out of pique, named Odysseus, who duly received Achilles' armor. That night Ajax, in a fit of madness, killed the entire flock of sheep intended to feed the Greeks, imagining it to be his enemies. In the morning, realizing the lengths to which he had been driven, he fell on this sword and committed suicide.

ALCMAEON

Like many of the Greek heroes, Alcmaeon found himself in difficulties through no fault of his own. His father was the prophet Amphiaraus, who knew that if he participated in the war of the Seven Against Thebes he would die. He therefore concealed himself but his whereabouts were betrayed by his wife, Eriphyle, who was seduced by the gift of a magnificent gold necklace by Polynices. Amphiaraus went to war, but told Alcmaeon that when he heard the news of his father's death, he should kill his mother in vengeance. This he duly did and was consequently pursued by the Furies (like ORESTES) because of his matricide. He was able to receive purification from the river god Phlegeus, whose daughter Alphesiboea he married and to whom he gave his mother's necklace. His land, however, was struck with barrenness and another oracle said that he had to be purified once again, but this time by the river god Achelous. After much wandering he found the god, who purified him and gave him his daughter Callirhoe in marriage. She demanded as a gift the famous necklace. Alcmaeon, in a quandry, retrieved the object from his first wife, Alphesiboea, upon the pretext of having to dedicate it to APOLLO at Delphi in final atonement for the murder of his mother. His father-in-law Phlegeus agreed to this, but subsequently found out the truth of the matter. He therefore had his sons murder Alcmaeon, whose body was left unburied and a prey to the wild animals. Alcmaeon's sons by Callirhoe then avenged their father's murder by killing his murderers.

AMMUT

Egyptian underworld goddess. Upon the physical death of a person a number of entities still continued to live. One element known as the Ateh descended into the Underworld where it negotiated dangerous paths, lakes of fire and doorways guarded by ferocious armed dieties and eventually came into the Hall of the Two Truths. There a tribunal of 42 gods examined the dead man's earthly life to judge if he deserved to spend eternity in the realm of OSIRIS. This entailed the heart, considered to be the record of all past deeds, being weighed in a pair of scales against the goddess of Truth. Provided the dead man's statements were truthful the scales balanced and the god THOTH declared him 'True of voice' and fit for the kingdom of Osiris. Ammut sat by the scales during the proceedings. She had the head of a crocodile, the body of a lion or leopard and the rear-end of a hippopotamus, and devoured those hearts that failed the examination, causing all other parts of the soul to perish. Her name is usually translated as 'Devouress of the Dead' or 'She who gobbles down'.

Left The savage Egyptian underworld god Ammut waits to devour the hearts of those who fail the test of the scales. Anubis, the jackal-headed god, carries out the test and Maet, goddess of truth, looks on.

Right Amun shown as a ferocious ram, from an Egyptian mummy case.

Below These ram-headed sphinxes sacred to Amun-Re line the avenue leading to the temple of Amun at Karnak (ancient Thebes). Each sphinx protects an image of the pharoah.

AMUN

An Egyptian deity who combined with the sun god to become Amun-Re (see RE), Amun was paramount in the Egyptian pantheon during the height of the pharaonic empire. He was an anthropomorphic god sporting a crown of two tall plumes. His name means 'the Hidden One' and gives little clue to his vital personality. He was also a war god, instigating attack and an impregnable bulwark for the defence of the royal warrior, being particularly associated with the military operations of Tuthmosis 111 (1479-1425 BC), when Egyptian dominion stretched from the Sudan to Syria, and with the less successful campaign of Rameses 11 (1290-1224 BC) against the Hittites. Scenes on the walls of the temples of Deir el Bahri and Luxor stress this close relationship. The most magnificent of the many temples dedicated to Amun was that of Karnak at Eastern Thebes; every year the New Year festival procession left the precinct of Karnak to travel by road and river to Luxor, with the statue of Amun towed on a splendid 100-foot gilded barge.

ANIATH see BAAL

ANDRO-MEDA

In Greek myth the daughter of Cepheus, King of Ethiopia, and Cassiopia. She claimed to be more beautiful than all the Nereids together, so they called upon POSEIDON to avenge this slur upon them. He sent a sea monster to ravage the land and the oracle of Ammon, when approached, said that the beast could only be appeased by offering Andromeda to it. She was consequently chained to a rock to await the monster. At the time PERSEUS, mounted on his flying horse PEGASUS, was returning from dealing with the GORGON and saw the girl. He fell in love with her and offered her father to free her if she married him. This was agreed and he straightway displayed the Gorgon head to the monster and turned it to stone. The couple returned to Argos and subsequently to Tiryns and had several sons.

Other versions of the legend locate Cepheus' kingdom in Phoenicia, on the Palestine coast and the rock Andromeda was chained to at Joppa (now covered by modern Tel Aviv).

Below This relief from the Rameseum at Luxor shows Rameses 11 before Amun, who is wearing his plumed crown and is supported by his consort Mut.

ANTIGONE   ANUBIS

Daughter of the Greek king OEDIPUS by his incestuous union with his mother Jocasta, Antigone was the epitome of the dutiful daughter and sister. When her father realized his great crime and blinded himself in remorse, she traveled with him around the countryside until his death. Returning then to Thebes in Boeotia she lived with her sister Ismene and found, in the war of the Seven Against Thebes, that her two brothers Eteocles and Polynices, were on opposing sides. They met in combat before the gates of Thebes and killed each other. Antigone's uncle Creon, who had usurped the throne of Thebes when Oedipus was disgraced, buried Eteocles in the proper manner but, since Polynices had introduced foreign troops on to Greek soil, his body was denied burial.

Against Creon's orders Antigone buried Polynices and was condemned by Creon to be walled up alive for disregarding his orders. She hanged herself and her fiancé, Creon's son Haemon, killed himself over her corpse while Creon's wife, Eurydice, committed suicide in desperation.

Egyptian jackal god responsible for the processes of embalming and the protection of the desert necropolis. The black coat of Anubis contrasts with the natural tawny colour of jackals to indicate the idea of resurrection in the next life, on the analogy of the life-supporting fertility of the Nile silt. It also hinted at the darkening hue of corpses after mummification. His association with the funerary cult may have originated with the depredations of jackals, hyenas and desert dogs in predynastic burial-grounds. As 'The one in front of the gods' pavilion' Anubis presided over the embalming tent while as 'Lord of the Sacred Land' his jurisdiction over the tombs was acknowledged. He dispensed the necessary fragrant oils for the embalmers to rub into the corpses and was also responsible for the wrapping of the body in linen bandages woven by the goddess Tayet. Beyond the tomb Anubis guided the deceased in the Underworld towards the throne of OSIRIS once the Weighing of the Heart ceremony had been successfully got through (see AMMUT).

Right   Anubis weighs the heart of the dead man to see if he deserves to remain in the kingdom of Osiris, from a thirteenth century BC tomb papyrus.

Left Egyptian deities continued to be worshipped well into the Roman period; this statue of the jackal-headed god Anubis probably dates from the first century BC.

ANZU (or Zu)

Also Imdugud, the Thunderbird of Sumerian mythology, a gigantic lion-headed bird-like figure who was conceived as a manifestation of the gods Ningirsu and later NINURTA. A famous relief discovered in a Sumerian temple at Ubaid in southern Iraq, which dates to the early third millenium BC gives a good idea of his appearance. This mythological figure was responsible for stealing the Tablet of Destinies from ENLIL, later recovered by Ninurta, in a myth attested in Sumerian and Akkadian versions.

APHRODITE

Greek goddess of love and beauty, the daughter of ZEUS by Dione. The best known account of her birth has her rising from the sea foam at Paphos on the coast of Cyprus (best epitomized in Botticelli's famous painting *The Birth of Venus* in the Uffizi, Florence). She was married to the smith god HEPHAESTUS, but left him for the war god

Far left above Delightfully informal drawing of Aphrodite and Pan playing knuckle bones, incised with a metal point on the back of a bronze mirror dating from the fourth century BC.

Far left below Aphrodite rising from the waves, as shown on the fifth century BC Greek Ludovisi throne.

Left The bull god Apis shown with the solar disc between his horns, in the Theban *Papyrus of Ani* from the *Book of the Dead*.

Below Apis with the four sons of Horus.

ARES, by whom she had five children, EROS being the best known. Among her other lovers were ADONIS and Anchises, by whom she had AENEAS.

Her favors lay with the Trojans during the Trojan War and especially with Aeneas. Her award of the Apple of Discord in the Judgment of PARIS between the goddesses HERA, Aphrodite, and ATHENA led to the abduction of HELEN, and the cause of the Trojan War. She was particularly prone to angry outbursts and gods as well as mortals suffered because of it.
See also VENUS.

APIS

In Egyptian mythology the creator god PTAH of Memphis had as his herald the bull-god Apis to communicate with mankind on his behalf in the delivery of oracles. Memphis was the administrative and political capital of Egypt so the cult of the Apis bull became the most prestigious animal cult in the land. The birth of the Apis bull was a miraculous event – its mother, the ISIS cow as she came to be called, conceived her calf through being struck by lightning. Traditionally the Apis bull bore particular markings consisting of a completely black hide except for a white triangle on its forehead, and the tip of its tail dividing into two thick strands. Its divinity was enhanced by a garment on its back in the design of the wings of a vulture goddess.

Above The fourth century BC temple of Apollo at Delphi was located on the remains of earlier temples, the site of the oracle.

APOLLO

Greek god, the son of LETO by ZEUS, had ARTEMIS as his slightly older twin sister. They were born on the island of Delos under the shade of the only tree that grew on it, a palm. The Roman traveler Pausanias said that there was a symbolic bronze palm tree in the sanctuary of Apollo when he visited Delos in the second century AD.

Apollo's major shrine was at Delphi, but before this could be established he first had to vanquish a monster, a dragon or serpent called Python, which terrorized the countryside. He slew the creature but to pacify its spirit inaugurated the Pythian Games at Delphi in its honor. Delphi became noted throughout the Ancient World for the oracular pronouncements made by the priestess, the Pythia, in a hallucinatory state (possibly achieved by chewing bay laurel leaves). All levels of society sent there for advice, which was usually

Left This Roman mosaic from a villa in Sicily shows Apollo as a sun-god, with rays bursting from his head.

of an ambiguous nature for the supplicant to interpret as best he could. In the legends HERACLES once came to consult the oracle at Delphi and, dissatisfied with his answer, then attempted to steal the sacred tripod, emblem of Apollo. The god and the hero fought over the tripod (this is often depicted in ancient art on coins and pottery) but ZEUS separated them and the tripod remained at Delphi.

Apollo was also the god of music, fine arts, poetry and eloquence. Like his sister Artemis he was a hunter and together they slew with their arrows the children of NIOBE after she had insulted their mother Leto. As the god of music he presided over the nine Muses on Mount Parnassus. He was also a god of medicine, who could cure as well as attack. Responsibility for the plague that struck the Greeks at Troy (Apollo favored the Trojans) lay with him and he used it to force them to return the daughter of his priest Chryses. He had a number of encounters with mankind, working at times for kings as herdsman, and several love affairs with mortal girls and nymphs, a number of whom assumed other shapes in an endeavor to escape his attentions.

In later legend he was closely associated with ORPHEUS and thereby with an eternal life concept.

Left The romanticized head of the Apollo Belvedere, a Roman copy of a Greek original, showing the god of music as an idealized human figure.

APOPHIS

In Egyptian mythology a gigantic serpent whose nature symbolized the idea of chaos and non-existence which all Egyptians dreaded. When RE the sun god descended behind Bakhu, the mountain of the west, to travel the twelve hours of night through the Underworld, Apophis lay in wait in order to swallow him. The sun god was towed along the Underworld waters on a boat but his crew became hypnotised by the stare of Apophis. The rescuer of Re was the god SETH whose strength matched that of Apophis who was subdued by a magical chant.

Below Heracles, who before he undertook his Twelve Labors accompanied Jason as one of the Argonauts, is shown on this sixth century BC Greek amphora removing the three-headed hound Cerberus from the Underworld.

ARES

Greek god of war, the son of ZEUS and his wife HERA. His brother was HEPHAESTUS the smith god. Always represented armed, he was prone to launch himself into a cause without enquiring too closely as to its validity. He was often at loggerheads with his half-sister ATHENA and in the Trojan War they supported different sides, he favoring the Trojans. He had a daughter, Harmonia, as a result of his affair with APHRODITE, who married CADMUS, king of Thrace, an area particularly associated with Ares. Most of his children by mortal women were of a violent nature.

The hill in Athens where religious crimes were tried in antiquity, the Areopagus, takes its name from the fact that Ares was tried there for the murder of Halirrhotius and acquitted by the Olympian gods on a verdict of what today would be called 'justifiable homicide'.

See also MARS.

ARGONAUTS

The name given to the crew of the ship *Argo* who accompanied JASON to Colchis on his quest for the Golden Fleece. Several catalogues of the participants exist but the two main ones are by Apollodorus and Apollonius of Rhodes, the latter being the better known. The *Argo* was a 40-oared ship built at Pagasae in Thessaly by Argos. ATHENA supervized the construction and herself brought a piece of oak from Zeus' sacred oak at Dodona to be carved into the prow, to which she gave the power of speech. This was to prove extremely useful on the voyage, since it was able to warn Jason of impending problems en route.

The crew included several well-known names such as HERACLES and the DIOSCURI. Jason is generally the prime mover and focus of most of their adventures, especially in his association with MEDEA and CIRCE.

The voyage of the Argonauts went up into the Black Sea to Colchis, where the quest was fulfilled, and then followed a circuitous route home that included southern Italy, North Africa and Crete. The whole episode lasted four months and, after they had arrived back at Iolchos with the Golden Fleece, Jason then sailed the *Argo* to Corinth, where it was dedicated to POSEIDON. The story is a navigational epic which has parallels in other mythologies, particularly Celtic. Its origins are earlier than the *Odyssey*, which refers to it, and it gives a great deal of important background to the Greek world of the time.

ARIADNE

Daughter of MINOS, King of Crete, and PASI-PHAE. In the legend of THESEUS she fell in love with him when he came with the other tribute youths and maidens from Athens to Crete to be sent into the Labyrinth to the MINOTAUR. Theseus promised to marry her if she helped him. She gave him a ball of thread and a sword, the former to be paid out as he entered the Labyrinth to help him find his way out after he had killed the Minotaur. Theseus succeeded and left Crete with Ariadne. However, he abandoned her on the island of Naxos, leaving her sleeping on the shore. DIONYSOS, the god of wine, passing by, was captivated by her beauty, woke her and married her. They are often represented together on Greek wine drinking vessels.

Above This Roman wall painting from Herculaneum shows Ariadne awaking on Naxos to find herself deserted by Theseus.

Left The story of Ariadne ends happily; Dionysus and his followers rescue her from her solitude, as shown on this fifteenth century Italian medallion.

ARTEMIS

Right This gold pectoral from the ancient town of Kamiros on Rhodes shows Artemis in her role as mistress of the animals.

Daughter of the Greek god ZEUS and LETO, and the slightly older twin sister of Apollo, born on the island of Delos. She was the eternal virgin huntress goddess but she had a somewhat vindictive nature and the deaths of a number of people were due to her, e.g. ACTAEON, Callisto, MELEAGER (indirectly through instigating the Calydonian Boar hunt), the children of NIOBE and Orion. In revenge for Agamemnon's boast at Aulis that he had killed a fine stag (Artemis' animal), she becalmed the Greek fleet until IPHIGENIA had been brought to be sacrificed to her.

At Ephesus, Artemis was worshiped more as the Asiatic mother goddess than the Greek huntress goddess, although stags were still associated with her as her familiar, as also were bees. Her temple there was listed as one of the Seven Wonders of the Ancient World and her cult statue, of which numerous later copies exist, was a curious herm-like statue noted for its many breasts and *polos* headdress.

See also DIANA.

Below The divine twins Apollo and Artemis shown shoulder to shoulder in the battle of the gods and giants, a detail from the frieze of the Siphnian treasury at Delphi.

ASCLEPIUS

Or Aesculapius, son of Coronis, whose father Phlelegyas was King of Thessaly, and the Greek god APOLLO. The god seduced the girl but then became angry when he found she had a mortal lover. He caused her death by lightning but saved the child, whom he gave to the centaur CHIRON to educate in the art of medicine. He was an exceptional pupil and was even able to bring the dead back to life, by using blood from the right side veins of the GORGON given him by ATHENA. PLUTO, god of the dead, complained to his brother ZEUS, who was not prepared to allow this situation to continue and he therefore struck Asclepius with a thunderbolt. Apollo was incensed at the death of this son but could do nothing against Zeus, so instead he killed the Cyclops who had made the thunderbolt.

After his death, Asclepius received divine honors and was changed into a constellation. His most famous shrine was at Epidauros where there are still extensive remains today, especially a magnificent theater. A number of gods from other religions were assimilated with him in the classical period, e.g. the Egyptian IMHOTEP.

Above This view of the great theater at Epidaurus shows the healing sanctuary of Asclepius in the background.

Left Asclepius was usually portrayed by the Greeks as a solemn bearded figure, as in this statue found at Piraeus, the port of Athens.

ASTARTE see ISHTAR

ATALANTA

Greek princess with various parents, according to the legends, but probably the best claim is that of Schoenus, King of Boeotia. Her father wanted only boys so she was abandoned at birth and fed by a she-bear until found by hunters, who brought her up. Wishing to remain a virgin, she dedicated herself to the huntress goddess ARTEMIS. She was present at the great Calydonian Boar hunt with the other heroes and is said to have been the first to wound it. Its head was given to her as a present by MELEAGER, who actually killed it and was himself to perish shortly after.

Such was her beauty that Atalanta had many suitors but she rejected them all, on the grounds either of her vow or that she had been told that, should she marry, she would be changed into an animal. To dissuade suitors she agreed to marry only he who could outrun her; any who failed, and she gave them a start, forfeited their lives, and many did. A fresh suitor, Melanion (sometimes given as Hippomanes), however, had her measure. APHRODITE had given him three golden apples from the Garden of the Hesperides. These he took to the contest with him and as soon as he felt Atalanta gaining on him in the race, he dropped the apples one by one. She stopped to pick them up, either out of avarice or perhaps because she wished to let him win. He won the race and her hand in marriage. Sometime later, while out hunting together, the pair entered a sanctuary of ZEUS (some legends say CYBELE) and there made love. Affronted at such sacrilege, Zeus changed them both into lions, thus fulfilling Atalanta's fear concerning marriage.

Below The warrior maiden Atalanta, on a late Roman mosaic from Tunisia.

ATEN

Briefly the ascendant deity in Egyptian mythology, his name means the 'disk of the sun'. His cult saw worship of a creator-god approaching close to (but not quite reaching) monotheism. The iconography of the god Aten took the form of the solar disk with rays emanating from it which ended in hands. Those hands approaching figures of royalty were depicted as holding 'signs of life'. It was during the reign of the pharaoh Tuthmosis IV (1401-1391 BC) that Aten begins his rise towards ascendant deity and the god's progress continued during the subsequent reign of Amenhotep III (1391-1353 BC) after which the traditional pantheon led by RE was re-established.

ATHENA

Greek goddess of wisdom, the daughter of Metis by ZEUS, she had a strange birth. Zeus had been warned that should Metis give birth to a daughter, she would be followed by a son who would take over Zeus' sphere. To thwart the prophecy, Zeus swallowed the infant just as Metis was about to give birth. He then developed a headache, so HEPHAESTUS took a double axe (labrys) and split his skull open and out leapt the goddess Athena, fully grown and armed.

Athens, Athena's premier city and sanctuary, with the Parthenon built on its Acropolis, was won by the goddess in a contest with POSEIDON. They contested the sovereignty of Attica and it was decided that whoever produced the better gift for mankind would be declared the winner. Poseidon struck a rock with his trident and a horse sprang forth (some versions say it was a salt-water spring on the Acropolis); Athena caused an olive tree to grow there. The gods judged the olive was the best gift and Athena won Athens.

As a warlike goddess she was the protector of many towns and heroes. In the Trojan War she sided with the Greeks because she could not forgive PARIS for not awarding her the golden apple. She especially watched over ACHILLES and ODYSSEUS, helping them both during the war and ODYSSEUS also during the course of his ten-year journey home to Ithaca afterward. Although she supported the Greeks it was an ancient form of her image as Pallas, referred to as the Palladium, that kept Troy safe while it remained in the city. Hence the reason why Odysseus and DIOMEDES stole it one night.

Her familiar bird was the owl which, with her head, became the city badge of the coins of

Above This famous fifth century BC marble relief shows Athena in her warrior helm mourning a dead hero.

Left The owl of Athena was adopted as an emblem by the city of Athens and appeared on many coins.

Right Athena as a protector goddess, probably a copy of the vast cult statue by the famous Greek sculptor Phidias, which does not survive. It was intended to stand in the Parthenon.

Athens. Her breastplate was the aegis made of goatskin and on the front of her shield she carried the head of the Gorgon, MEDUSA, which PERSEUS had given her.

See also MINERVA.

ATLAS

A giant in Greek myth, the son of the sea nymph Clymene and Iapetus. By his wife Pleione, daughter of Oceanus, he had seven children. He fought against the gods in the great battle between gods and giants and as punishment ZEUS condemned him to carry the sky on his shoulders. He is also said to have been a king in North Africa who refused hospitality to PERSEUS upon his return from slaying the Gorgon, MEDUSA. Perseus therefore showed him Medusa's head and turned him to stone, thus creating the Atlas Mountains that stretch across North Africa.

ATRA-HASIS

'Exceedingly-Wise' hero of the Akkadian *Atra-hasis* myth first attested in cuneiform tablets of the seventeenth century BC, which began 'When the gods like man . . .'. The story, still partly unrecovered, tells of the period in the mists of ancient time before the appearance of man, when the gods had to fend for themselves. The junior gods responsible for the harder work rebeled, and so the chief gods decided to create mankind to do the work for them. Enki and the principal mother goddess made a man out of clay like a figurine, animated with flesh and blood taken from an obscure god called We-ila, and with their divine saliva. Having produced the human prototype, a group of mother goddesses worked to make seven males and seven females. A brick structure mentioned in this connection evidently corresponds to the brick birth couch used in Mesopotamian society.

Above The tholos of Athena at Delphi, built in the fourth century BC. Circular temples were relatively unusual in classical Greece and there is some doubt as to their function.

The human race, once set on its path, multiplied rapidly, to the point that the hubbub disturbed the gods, who were prompted to turn to desperate remedies. Plague, drought and famine were unsuccessfully tried by ENLIL to dispose of the human nuisance, but each time he was foiled by Enki, who was determined on protecting the human race through the king, Atra-hasis. Finally Enlil resolved to destroy mankind with a flood. The description of the Flood in this myth is closely related to, and indeed provided the source for, that in the GILGAMESH Epic. Atra-hasis, guided by Enki (who communicated with him deviously as he had been banned from interfering further), built a boat from the reeds of his house, and sealed it with pitch. He then took on board his family, goods and chattels, and healthy examples of animals and birds, before the flood waters arrived, destroying all life on earth. Rain fell for seven days and nights, and the interruption of their regular offerings made some of the gods regret their hasty decision to dispense with their human servants. The description of the settling of the boat and decline of the waters in the Gilgamesh version is still missing from the sources for this myth. Once landed Atra-hasis craftily sacrificed at once to the hungry gods, who were attracted 'like flies' to the smell of the food. Enlil, annoyed still at the survival of Enki's protegé, insisted on strict measures to prevent similar noise in the future by arranging for the existence of various classes of women banned from having children.

Below This wine jar from Mycenae dates from the Heroic Period, the twelfth century BC, and with its exquisite marine decoration reflects the sea-going ambitions of the mainland Greek kings.

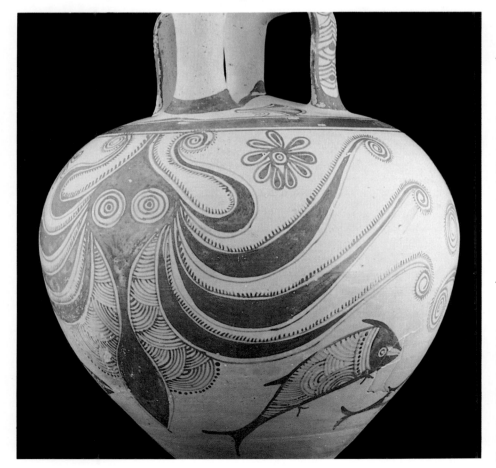

ATREUS

In Greek myth, the father of AGAMEMNON and MENELAUS (often therefore called the Atridae). He had been the King of Pisa but, having been involved in the murder of his half-brother Chrysippus, he had fled to Mycenae where he married Aerope, daughter of King Eurystheus, whom he succeeded on the throne. The family history then becomes horrendous and complicated. Atreus' brother, Thyestes, followed him to Mycenae and had an affair with his wife, Aerope. Having found out about it, Atreus pretended to forgive his brother and invited him to a banquet. He served a dish of stewed meat and after Thyestes had eaten it Atreus displayed to him the heads of his three sons who had been killed and their flesh served to their father. Thyestes fled to the court of Sicyon, where, without knowing her identity, he fathered a son, Aegisthus, on his own daugher Pelopea. Shortly afterwards she married Atreus, his own wife having died. Atreus adopted Aegisthus without knowing who his father was and sent him to murder Thyestes. Thyestes knew that Aegisthus was his own son and revealed himself; Aegisthus therefore changed tack and returned to Mycenae and murdered Atreus. A large tholos tomb at Mycenae is called the 'Treasury of Atreus' although it has no known connection with him.

ATROPOS

One of the Three Fates (the Moirai to the Greeks; to the Romans they were the Parcae), along with her sisters CLOTHO and LACHESIS. They were the daughters of ZEUS and Themis, goddess of Law. Atropos was the eldest sister, who snipped through the thread of each man's life with a pair of scissors.

ATUM

In Egyptian mythology one form that the sun god RE was thought to take was that of Atum 'Lord of Heliopolis', a primeval creator god. Self-engendered he rose up out of the primeval water, an analogy with the Nile inundation, and masturbated. The falling semen transmuted into the air-god SHU and the moisture-goddess TEFNUT who in turn produced the earth god GEB and the sky goddess NUT.

Left The Lion Gate is the main entrance to the great Greek citadel of Mycenae, whence Helen was stolen by Paris.

BACCHUS

Son of JUPITER and SEMELE and the Roman equivalent of the Greek god of wine DIONYSUS. He shared the same attributes and most of the legends of his precursor. In the Roman world, and especially in Roman North Africa, he was often known as LIBER PATER, after an old Italian god. The Bacchanalia, an orgiastic and drunken celebration of the god, reached such heights that it had to be banned by the Roman Senate in 186 BC.

Far left The maenads, wild followers of the wine god Bacchus, join in a riotous Bacchic procession on this Roman sarcophagus.

Left Canaanite bronze deity in the attitude of Baal, with arm upraised to hold a spear representing lightning.

Below Bacchus on his leopard is accompanied by his principal follower Silenus, mounted on a donkey.

Bottom This early third century AD mosaic from Sousse in Tunisia shows the triumph of Bacchus; a winged Victory stands behind him, and vines curl riotously in every direction.

BAAL

This name, the general Semitic word for 'lord', 'master', is applied especially to Baal-Hadad, the Canaanite storm and weather god, and indeed king of the gods, well known from the mythological texts of the second millennium BC from Ugarit (Ras Shamra). Of probable West-Semitic or Amorite origin, he is described in Ugaritic texts as 'most powerful of heroes', and 'the one who rides the clouds'. He was the son of Dagon, and brother to the 'virgin' Anath, and hero of a great and complicated mythological epic, written over seven cuneiform tablets.

A great temple was built for him, but Baal was slain by monsters and carried off to the Land of Death. As a result all life on earth was grievously affected, so Anath found Mot, the god of death, and slaughtered him after a fierce battle. Mot's body was cut up, winnowed, burned, ground up and sowed in the ground and by this means Baal was revived.

Above Norse horned god represented on a gold horn found at Gallehus, Sweden.

BALDER

Called the Beautiful, he was the son of the Norse god ODIN and his wife FREYA. Despite these illustrious parents, he was essentially an obscure god – some say that he was only an elevated human hero and not a god. The two best accounts of him, which differ considerably in the manner of his death, are given in *The Danish History* by Saxo Grammaticus and the *Prose Edda* by Snorri Sturluson, an Icelandic writer who lived from 1179 to 1241.

Balder personified all that was best in youth: he was blond and beautiful, wise, brave in battle and gracious in his living. The story of his life, and especially the manner of his death, is among the most moving of the Northern myths. The details are of particular interest in the close similarities to many of the earlier myths of the ancient Near East and gods such as ADONIS, ATIS, OSIRIS and TAMMUZ.

Odin and Freya loved Balder so much that Freya extracted a promise from all things that none of them would harm Balder; he was thus invulnerable to weapons. In battle none could overcome him, especially his adversary, the human hero Hoder. Both loved the same maiden, Nanna, and the myths seem agreed that it was Hoder who finally married her.

On account of his invulnerability, the gods would often play games with Balder and while he stood quietly they would hurl all manner of objects at him which, naturally, caused him no harm but created amusement for all. However, the scheming and mischievous god LOKI, who was jealous of Balder's popularity, determined to bring about his downfall.

Balder began to have frightening dreams which caused the gods some anxiety. Therefore, his father Odin rode down into the underworld to seek the advice of a long dead seeress who could interpret the dreams for him. She predicted the death of Balder and said that it would be caused by the blind god HODER (not to be confused with the human hero of the same name). She went on to say that Hoder himself would subsequently die at the hands of a son of Odin yet to be born. Her predictions caused concern, but the gods largely ignored them because of Balder's invulnerability. However, they had reckoned without the jealous Loki. He had found that just one thing had not given its promise to Freya not to harm Balder, and that was the humble mistletoe growing on the great oak tree. Loki made a sharp dart out of a sprig of mistletoe and then waited his chance. It soon came when the gods were next playing and throwing things at Balder. The blind Hoder stood nearby, not taking part. Loki approached him and said that he should join in the sport. Hoder could not see so Loki gave him the dart of mistletoe and offered to guide Hoder's throw. It was all too effective; Balder was struck, pierced by the dart and fell dead. The gods were distraught at losing him but found that if all living things would agree to weep for Balder, he could be restored to life. Odin went around and asked this of everyone with success, until he came across an old woman, Thokk, who refused to weep for the dead god – she was Loki in disguise. So they lost their darling and the lives of the gods of the North were never so bright again.

The myth of Balder is actually very complex in its overtones of the dying god/hero and much has been made by writers such as Sir James Frazer in his book *The Golden Bough* concerning the use of mistletoe as the deadly weapon.

BASTET

Originally in Egyptian mythology a lioness, who modified into the more benign cat goddess in the first millennium BC. In her early occurrences Bastet, as daughter of RE the sun-god, was a royal protectress; her name is carved on the northern facade of the granite valley temple of King Khafre at Giza, counterbalancing the southern goddess HATHOR. In the north-east Delta there once stood an impressive temple with ceremonial halls of granite which was sacred to Bastet. This temple at Bubastis once witnesed riotous festivals of music and dancing described in the fifth century BC by the Greek historian Herodotus. Sacred cats kept near the temples were buried in cemeteries and cats were revered in the household. Mummified cats were frequently elaborately wrapped with the linen bandages forming geometric patterns. The Ancient Egyptian sense of humor comes across in the faces painted on these cat mummies expressing bewilderment, indignation or an enchanting smile.

Left This bronze statue of the Egyptian goddess Bastet shows her in her benign feline aspect, together with kittens. She could also be represented as a lioness.

Right The hero Bellerophon, mounted on Pegasus, kills the dreaded Chimaera; this fifth century BC Greek statue shows clearly the flame-throwing goat's head which sprouted from the middle of the monster's back.

Right This first century AD Roman wall painting from Pompeii shows Bellerophon taming the great winged horse Pegasus.

BELLERO-PHON

Greek hero son of Glaucus, King of Corinth, and Eurymede. In his youth, Bellerophon accidentally killed a man and had to leave Corinth. He made his way to Tiryns (an old Mycenaean citadel in Argos) and the court of King Proteus, who purified him of the murder. Unfortunately, the king's wife Anteia (also known as Stheneboea) made advances to him and, when he rejected her, she accused him of trying to seduce her. Her husband could not avenge the charge as Bellerophon was his guest, so he sent him to his father-in-law Iobates, King of Lycia and Anteia's father, with a sealed letter asking that the bearer be killed. Iobates, reading it and believing the charge made against Bellerophon, sent him to kill the Chimaera. This was a monstrous beast, part lion, part dragon, and with a flame-throwing goat's head sprouting from the middle of its back, which was laying waste the countryside. Bellerophon found the winged horse PEGASUS drinking at the Pirene spring in Corinth and captured it. He was thus able successfully to attack the Chimaera, avoiding its dangerous goat's head, and kill it.

In a second attempt to have Bellerophon killed, Iobates sent him against his warlike neighbors the Solymi. This also failed, as did the next one against the Amazons. Finally, an ambush was laid by the best of the Lydian warriors, but they also fell to Bellerophon. The king realized that the gods were protecting the innocent and he gave Bellerophon his daughter Philonoe in marriage and made him heir to the kingdom of Lycia. A late aspect of the legend says that Bellerophon, in old age, tried to ride his winged horse into the lands of the gods. For his presumption ZEUS hurled him back into the sea, where he was drowned.

Left The legend of Bellerophon and Pegasus had wide appeal; this exquisitely engraved bronze cista is Etruscan and dates from about 300 BC.

BELLONA

The Roman goddess of war, often associated with MARS as his wife, sometimes as his sister. Her Greek equivalent was Enyo, often represented covered in blood. Bellona was sometimes shown on the reverse types of Roman Republican silver coins (*denarii*).

BEOWULF

The hero of one of the longest poems, and certainly the most important, to have survived complete in Old English. His name is properly Beowulf of the Geats (a Swedish tribe). The poem was composed in about the eighth century AD and the sole surviving manuscript of some 3000 lines (now in the British Library) dates from c 1000 AD. It was written down by two scribes, as is evident by the differences in handwriting and spelling.

Beowulf was the nephew of Hygelac, King of the Geats. Hearing of the problems that his friend the Dane Hrothgar was having with a half-human monster called Grendel, he decided to help him. Hrothgar had built his hall at Heorot, close to the monster's lair in the fens, and it took exception to the sound of revelry. Grendel attacked the hall by night and killed 30 of the Danes, and repeated his raids at intervals over the following 12 years. Beowulf sailed for Denmark from Sweden with 14 of his men and one night, after the feasting in the hall was finished, they remained to await the monster's attack. Grendel arrived, burst in at the door and immediately killed one of the Geats, then turned on Beowulf. After a mighty struggle Beowulf ripped off one of its arms and the monster fled, mortally wounded, back to its fenland lair. A great feast followed at which Beowulf and his men were fêted and received many gifts. After the banquet, as everyone slept, Grendel's mother raided the hall bent on avenging her dead son and carried off one of Hrothgar's councillors. At first light, Geats and Danes tracked her to the lake in which she lived. Beowulf plunged into the depths and, after a mighty struggle, killed the monster. Finding Grendel's corpse in the depths of the lake he cut off its head and returned in triumph to Heorot, where another great feast was laid on.

Beowulf returned home to Sweden and presented his trophies to his king, Hrothgar, receiving rich gifts in return. Subsequently, after the death of Hrothgar and his son Heardred in war, Beowulf became King of the Geats. After a rule of some 50 years, a dragon attacked his country and the old hero turned out to combat the peril to his people. Alone with his kinsman Wiglaf, the other followers having fled, the two faced the dragon and eventually killed it, but Beowulf was mortally wounded and died in Wiglaf's arms as he berated the cowards. The Geats pushed the dragon's corpse over a cliff edge into the sea and built a huge funeral pyre for Beowulf, erecting a burial mound over it into which they placed both Beowulf and the dragon's treasure.

At both the beginning and the end of the poem there is a funeral. At the beginning there is the ship burial of the old King Scyld, mythical founder of the present Danish royal family; at the end there is the cremation of Beowulf. Although the story line may seem rather naive, the details contained in the poem are of exceptional interest; much recently unearthed archaeological evidence bears out the descriptions in the poems of ceremonies, buildings and artifacts. The prime source has been the so-called cenotaph ship burial found at Sutton Hoo on the river Deben in Suffolk, England. It is generally thought to be the burial of the Saxon King Raedwald, c. 625 AD. Excavated in August 1939 just prior to the outbreak of the Second World War, it produced a fantastic treasure that is now in the British Museum. Subsequent re-excavation and a continuing programme of re-examination of the whole cemetery group of mounds under Professor Martin Carver has added more, but smaller, finds and much information.

BES

Egyptian deity particularly relevant to ordinary Egyptians since he was responsible for the prosperity of the family and in particular for the welfare of children. He is unmistakable in iconography in his form of a huge-bellied dwarf with bandy legs whose face is a hybrid of human and leonine characteristics. He can bare his fangs, protrude his tongue and brandish a dagger but all this aggression is directed to thwart evil forces that might endanger the family. His image decorated the walls of bedrooms, as indicated in the excavations of the village of workmen at Deir el Medina in Western Thebes. He also appeared on utilitarian objects such as head-rests, mirrors, and cosmetic spoons and tubes for eye paint and makeup. In Ptolemaic and Roman cult temples, such as the temple of Hathor at Dendera, an important element was the sanctuary celebrating the birth of the child of the principal god and goddess. Over the entrance the effigy of Bes was cut to ward off any hostile being from harming the divine child whose birth was celebrated inside.

BRUNHILDA

In Norse legend one of the Valkyrie, warrior priestesses of FREYA, whose role was to carry the souls of heroes killed in battle to ODIN in Asgard, to aid the gods in the final battle against the giants. Brunhilda defies Odin and as a punishment is condemned to sleep in a castle surrounded by flames until a human warrior braves the fire and wakes her, a form of initiation ceremony. She is finally woken by SIGURD and becomes betrothed to him, but he subsequently loses his memory and agrees to impersonate Gunnar so that Gunnar can win Brunhilda. When she discovers the deception she has Sigurd killed and then kills herself.

In the Icelandic saga the *Nibelunglied*, Brunhilda is a queen of Iceland who will only marry a hero who can defeat her in three trials of strength; again she is overcome by Siegfried (Sigurd) wearing a helmet of invisibility, but again she is deceived into marrying Gunther and has Siegfried murdered.

Below The Egyptian god Bes combined human and leonine characteristics in his role as protector of the family. This blue faience statue dates from the Roman period.

CADMUS

A Greek hero whose sister EUROPA was abducted by ZEUS in the shape of a bull. He was the son of Agenor, King of Phoenicia, and Telephassa. Cadmus' father sent him and his brothers in search of their sister, with orders not to return without her. The quest was impossible and an oracle suggested that Cadmus should found a city by following a cow until it stopped from exhaustion. He found a cow wandering off by itself which had the mark of the moon in white on each of its flanks. This he took to be an omen and followed it as directed. When the site for the city had been identified, Cadmus sent some of his companions to seek water to be used in a thank offering to the gods. Since they were a long time returning, he went in search of them and found they had been attacked by a dragon that guarded the pool. He slew it with ATHENA's assistance, who then said that he should sow the dragon's teeth. Immediately there sprang up a number of armed warriors who began advancing on Cadmus. Quickwittedly he hurled a large stone into their midst and they started fighting among themselves. The five that survived became his companions, one of them, Echion, ultimately marrying one of Cadmus' daughters, Agave.

Cadmus set about building the city, which became Thebes in Boeotia. Zeus gave him Harmonia, the daughter of APHRODITE by ARES, for his wife and he had a son, Polydorus and four daughters. One of them, SEMELE, was to become the mother of DIONYSUS by Zeus. In old age Cadmus and Harmonia left Thebes, some accounts say because of HERA's persecution of their children, and went to Illyrium. A prophecy had said that should they live there the Illyrians would be victorious over their rivals, the Encheleans. This came about and Cadmus ruled in Illyria, producing another son, Illyrius. Subsequently, Cadmus and his wife were changed into serpents who were sent to the Elysian Fields (the Greek heaven).

CALYPSO

A Greek nymph, the daughter of ATLAS and Pleione, who lived on the island of Ogygia in the western Mediterranean (actually the peninsula of Ceuta opposite Gibraltar). ODYSSEUS, in his wanderings after the fall of Troy, arrived there and Calypso fell in love with him. By her enchantment she was able to keep him with her for seven (perhaps ten) years. Eventually, on the plea of ATHENA, who always looked after Odysseus' interests, HERMES was sent by ZEUS to persuade Calypso to let him depart, which she did, providing Odysseus with wood for a raft and food for his journey.

CAMULOS

A Belgic war god who is equated with MARS in the classical pantheon. He was a god of the Remi, a Belgic tribe from the area of Rheims, and he appears to have entered Britain in his warlike aspect. His name is the root of the early town Camulodunum (Colchester in Essex) which means 'Fort of Camulos'. This city was the stronghold of Cunobelin, the British warrior chieftain and it was there, after the Roman Conquest in 43 AD, that the Emperor Claudius built a great temple to his own divinity. This and the city was sacked by the British Queen Boudica in the uprising of 60/61 AD.

Far left Three Celtic mother goddesses, each holding a dish of bread to indicate their role as fertility figures. The triple aspect is a common feature of Celtic mythology.

Below Central roundel of the Battersea Shield, a Celtic votive shield found in the River Thames which may well have been an offering to a war god such as Camulos. The swirling decoration is typical of the Celtic La Tène style.

CASSANDRA

Daughter of PRIAM, King of Troy, and Hecuba and beloved of APOLLO. She resisted his advances and he offered her the gift of prophecy if she would yield to him; however, having received the gift, she changed her mind and continued to refuse him. He could not withdraw the gift but he could change it; although she would prophesy accurately, Apollo decreed that no one would believe her. She foretold that PARIS would bring about the downfall of Troy and that HELEN's abduction would be the cause. When the Greeks made the Wooden Horse in an attempt to trick their way into the city, Cassandra and the priest Laocoon cried out against bringing it into the city. Hera sent snakes to destroy Laocoon and his family and no one believed Cassandra when she said the Horse was full of armed warriors.

At the fall of Troy, Cassandra took refuge at the statue of Athena, where she was found and dragged away by the Lesser AJAX, who committed sacrilege in this act. Cassandra became the property of AGAMEMNON when the spoils were divided and he took her back with him to Mycenae. She had prophesied that his wife, CLYTEMENSTRA, would kill him which she did, together with Cassandra.

CASTOR see DIOSCURI

CAUTES see MITHRAS

CAUTOPATES see MITHRAS

CERBERUS

The three-headed monster who in Greek myth guarded the entrance to Hades had curious parents. His father was the multiheaded giant

Below Greek vase showing the three-headed monster Cerberus being subdued by Heracles as one of his Twelve Labors. Athena and Hermes look on protectively as Heracles leads the creature out of the Underworld.

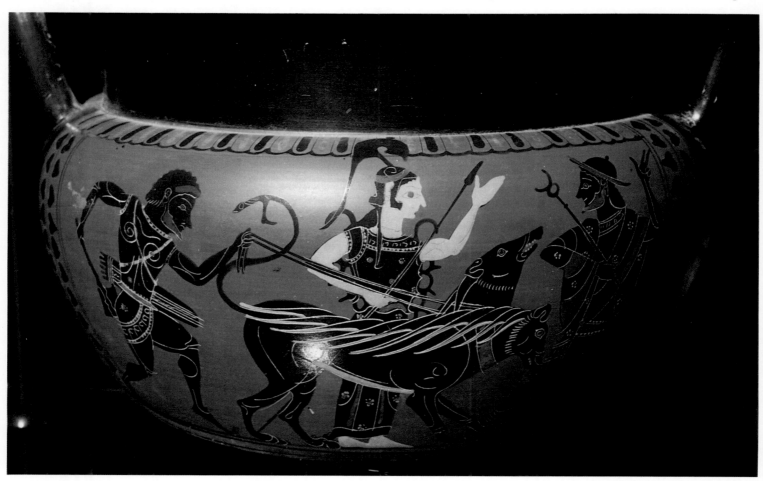

Left The Roman temple of Ceres at Ostia, the seaport near Rome, still has a suitably calm and rural atmosphere for a sanctuary belonging to the goddess of fertility and harvest.

Below Sixteenth century Italian plate showing Erisichthon, who impudently felled the sacred grove of Ceres. In punishment the goddess afflicted him with perpetual hunger; he squandered all his possessions in an attempt to assuage it and finally devoured his own limbs. The story is told in Ovid's *Metamorphoses*.

Typhon and his mother was Echidna, a beautiful woman above the waist but a serpent below. Cerberus' task was to prevent the living entering the kingdom of Hades and to make sure that none of the dead escaped from it. It was one of the Labours of HERACLES to bring Cerberus up from hell to earth to King Eurytheus, which he did with Hades' permission so long as he did not use any weapons to subdue the beast. Heracles half throttled all three heads and dragged him up before Eurytheus, who promptly dived into a large *pithos* (jar) in terror – a very popular scene in Greek vase painting. ORPHEUS charmed Cerberus with the music of his lyre and is the only person who passed in and out of hell, in his search for EURYDICE.

CERES

The Roman equivalent of the Greek DEMETER, the goddess of corn and the harvest. She shares the same legends and sanctuaries.

Right The Celtic horned god Cernunnos, surrounded by cult animals including a ram-headed serpent; detail from a Celtic silver cauldron found at Gundestrup, Denmark.

Below Cernunnos came to be worshiped by the Roman military stationed in formerly Celtic regions; this Roman-style relief was found in Rheims, France.

CERNUNNOS

The horned god, probably the oldest of the Celtic deities, who may even have origins in the horned god of the palaeolithic cave paintings. He is normally shown seated cross-legged, his distinctive horns on his head, and surrounded by animals. On the famous relief panel on the silver cauldron from Gundestrup, Denmark, he is shown wearing and also holding a torc, the characteristic Celtic neck-ring, in his right hand and a snake with a ram's head in his left. His aspect as a god holding sway over animals is emphasized here, as it is also on a relief from Rheims where he is shown squatting on an altar above a bull and a stag, with the classical gods MARS and APOLLO standing in subservient attitudes beside him. There are three important elements in his iconography – his horns, the wearing of a torc, and the cross-legged pose. A number of classical authors note this in relation to Celtic tribes, remarking that they were accustomed to squat since they did not have chairs. Not all Celtic gods found with apparent horns on their heads are representations of Cernunnos; often these are only stubs of wings, more appropriate to MERCURY's winged helmet.

CHARON

The ferryman who in Greek legend took the souls of the dead across the marshes of Acheron and the river Styx to hell. His parents were brother and sister, Erebus and Nox, the children of Chaos. He was represented as a disreputable, filthy old man with a straggly beard and tattered clothes who bullied the souls, his passengers; they not only had to pay his fee for the crossing but also row themselves. The fee, a small silver coin called an *obol*, was often put under the tongue of the corpse. When HERACLES went down into hell to retrieve CERBERUS, Charon refused him passage across the Styx but Heracles beat him so violently with his own ferryhook that he had to succumb. For allowing a living being into Hades, Charon was sentenced to be chained for a year.

Above In Greek myth the Chimaera was a monstrous creature, part lion and part dragon, with a flame-throwing goat's head in the middle of its back. It was finally killed by the hero Bellerophon.

Left Sixth century BC tombstone painting showing the ferryman Charon ferrying dead souls across the River Styx.

Above The battle between the Lapiths and the Centaurs, part of the sculptural decoration on the Parthenon, began at the wedding feast of the Lapith king Pirithous, where the centaurs, unaccustomed to wine, became offensively drunk and tried to rape the women guests.

CHIRON

The centaur, half man and half horse, was the son of CRONUS and Philyra. His curious form came about because his father had coupled with his mother in the shape of a horse. Chiron was born immortal but was always interested in and kindly towards humans. He was famous for his wisdom and his knowledge of music, medicine and ethics. Many of the great heroes of mythology were his pupils. These included ACHILLES, AENEAS, ASCLEPIUS, HERACLES, JASON and Peleus. Chiron was particularly famous for his medical knowledge and introduced surgery when he replaced a damaged bone in Achilles' ankle with a section from that of a giant.

Not all the centaurs were as amiable as Chiron. Some were rapacious and unruly, as the classic Battle between the Lapiths and Centaurs show (carved on reliefs from the Parthenon and the temple of Apollo at Bassae, Greece, now in the British Museum). At the Massacre of the Centaurs they were pursued by Heracles with his magic bow. Unfortunately Chiron, standing by Heracles, was accidentally wounded in the knee by an arrow. Even his medical skills with ointments could not heal a wound from Heracles' arrow. The pain was excruciating and Chiron retreated to a cave, imploring ZEUS to take away his immortality so that he could die. His wish was granted and he was placed among the constellations as Sagittarius, the Archer.

CIRCE

Greek princess noted for her command of the magic arts. She was the daughter of the Sun and Perseis and sister of Aeetes, King of Colchis (who kept the Golden Fleece retrieved by JASON) and of PASIPHAE, the wife of MINOS, King of Crete. She lived on the island of Aeaea, which is located near modern Monte Circeo, near Naples in Italy. ODYSSEUS made landfall near her palace and sent some men to reconnoiter. One, Eurylochus, more cautious than the rest, stayed back as the group was invited into the palace. They were feasted with meat and wine and then Circe touched each of them with her wand, changing them into various animals reflecting their individual natures. Eurylochus fled back to Odysseus and told him what he had seen.

Resolving to save his companions, Odysseus was making his way through the woods when he met the god MERCURY, who told him how to break Circe's spells. Odysseus was given a herb to put secretly into the wine Circe would give him. This would make him impervious to her spells and he was then to draw his sword and threaten her life. All worked as Mercury had said; Circe's spell was broken and, under threat of Odysseus' sword, she vowed not to harm any of the men and to change them back into their human form. They stayed a while with her, some accounts say a month, others ten years. The outcome was that Circe had two children by Odysseus, a son named Telegonus (who became the founder of Tusculum) and a daughter, Cassiphone.

Circe was also involved with JASON and the ARGONAUTS upon their return journey from Colchis. They landed there because Circe was MEDEA's aunt.

CLOTHO

The youngest of the three Fates, the Greek Moirai, Roman Parcae. Her sisters were ATROPOS and LACHESIS. They were the children of Zeus and Themis, goddess of law. Clotho was always represented with a distaff because it was she who spun the thread of man's life.

Left The sorceress Circe gives Odysseus a magic potion to make him her willing slave, a curiously folksy representation on a fifth century BC Theban vase. Circe had already transformed Odysseus' companions into pigs, but he managed to evade her magic and release his friends.

Above The city walls and the citadel of Mycenae looking north toward Mount Prophet Elias, where a signal fire would have warned Clytemnestra of Agamemnon's return.

CLYTEMNESTRA

A major figure in the story of the Trojan War. She was the daughter of Tyndareus, King of Sparta, and LEDA. HELEN was her half-sister and the Dioscuri her half-brothers by ZEUS and Leda. Her first husband was Tantalus, but he and their children were killed by AGAMEMNON, who then married her. When Agamemnon left for Troy with his brother MENELAUS, he left Clytemnestra in the care of his cousin, Aegisthus, who formed a liaison with her. When the Greek fleet was becalmed at Aulis, Agamemnon sent for his daughter IPHIGENIA because an oracle had decreed that she should be sacrificed for a fair wind. Agamemnon carried out the sacrifice, concealing his plans for murder from her mother, Clytemnestra. This, and her involvement with

Aegisthus, turned Clytemnestra against Agamemnon. Upon his return to Argos after the fall of Troy she plotted with Aegisthus to murder him. Together they killed him with axes after he had taken a bath and was struggling to put on a shirt that Clytemnestra had handed him with its sleeves sewn up. CASSANDRA, who had been brought from Troy as part of Agamemnon's share of the spoils, was also murdered by the pair. Clytemnestra's hatred then turned towards her children by Agamemnon. Her daughter ELECTRA was imprisoned at Mycenae but the boy ORESTES escaped and in later life returned, seeking vengeance for his father's murder. He killed his mother and her lover, and the FURIES then pursued him for his crime of matricide.

COCIDIUS

A Celtic god particularly associated with the area of Hadrian's Wall in Northern England, where at least eight dedications to him have been found. In the *Ravenna Cosmography* there is a place name listed as *Fanum Cocididi*, the temple of Cocidius, which seems to be close to the fort at Bewcastle, forward of the Wall, somewhere in the Irthing Valley. Excavations in the fort produced two important small silver plaques showing the god in relief, holding a spear and shield, with punched inscriptions *Deo Cocidio*. He is clearly a military god and is often linked with MARS on his dedications. He is also associated with Silvanus as a god of woodland and wildlife, and he shares an altar with him dedicated at Housesteads.

Left The Celtic god Cocidius shown in Romano-British guise as Silvanus the Hunter on a red jasper intaglio found near Hadrian's Wall.

COVENTINA

A water goddess or nymph best known from the Celtic dedication to her of a well outside the Roman fort of Carrawburgh on Hadrian's Wall. Her cult probably predates the Wall and was simply carried on into Roman times. When her well was cleared in 1876 it was found to be full of votive offerings; over 14 000 coins were recovered and also numerous altars dedicated to her. The coins and other votives were obviously thrown in as offerings but it seems that the altars were tipped in at a time of danger when the shrine was under attack and the goddess's well was thought to be the safest place for them. Water cults were very important in Celtic religion and Coventina is certainly the most famous of such deities known from the area of Hadrian's Wall.

Below Stone relief showing the Celtic water goddess Coventina in triple form, from Coventina's well at Carrawburgh.

CRONUS

SATURN to the Romans, was the youngest of the six Titans born to URANUS and GAIA. Incited by his mother, he castrated his father and took his place as king but continued in the same despotic way, so that Gaia plotted a second revolution. Cronus married his sister RHEA and began to produce children. However, Uranus and Gaia told him that he would be ovethrown by one of his own children, so he took to swallowing them as they were born. Five were dispatched in this way (Hestia, DEMETER, HERA, HADES and POSEIDON). With the coming of the sixth child, Rhea fled to Crete in an endeavor to protect it. The child, ZEUS, was born on Crete in the Dikte Cave; to deceive Cronus who came looking for him, Rhea gave him a stone heavily wrapped in cloths, which he swallowed. Zeus grew up in secrecy and then gave Cronus a potion that made him regurgitate the other five children. They all then declared war on Cronus and, with the aid of those children of Gaia that Cronus had imprisoned, they defeated and killed him and the second, major line of the Greek gods reigned with Zeus at their head.

Above Sixteenth century Italian plate painted by Giovanni Maria, showing Cupid riding on a dolphin and surrounded by mythical creatures. Italian artists of the fifteenth and sixteenth centuries found a new source of inspiration in classical mythology.

Right First century AD wall painting from Pompeii showing Cupid attending Mars and Venus.

LCORNELIVS·SCIPIOOREITVS
·VCAVGVRTAVROBOLIVM

Cronus was also the father of the centaur CHIRON by Philyra.

CUPID

The Roman god of love, equivalent to the Greek EROS, whose mother was Venus (Aphrodite) and his father variously given in the legends as Jupiter (Zeus), Mars (Ares), or Mercury (Hermes). He is usually represented as a small, chubby naked child armed with a bow and arrows. Mischievously, he would aim 'Cupid's darts' at will, at times causing untold mayhem as they caused those they pierced to fall in love with the first person they met. In classical art he is often shown playing a game such as quoits, but sometimes he wears a helmet and carries spear and shield to show that even Mars, god of war, gives way to love. His encounter with PSYCHE shows him in a more serious aspect.

CYBELE

Syrian mother or earth goddess, variously described as the mother and the lover of the resurrected god Atis. In one legend Atis was so harrased by the attentions of a loving monster that he castrated himself. In another version he was put to death because of his love for Cybele, daughter of the king of Phrygia and Lydia. Cybele equates with ISHTAR, ISIS and Rhea. Her sanctuary was at Pessinus in Phrygia and her priests were eunuchs. She was attended by lions, and the castration, death and rebirth of her consort was celebrated annually as part of the seasonal cycle of decay and regeneration. The ceremonies were bloody; rams were sacrificed and their blood used for baptism, and the initiates used the sickle-shaped knife associated with the goddess for ritual castration. The cult of Cybele was introduced into Rome in 205 BC and, like those of Isis and MITHRAS, attracted a considerable following.

Above The Syrian mother goddess Cybele in her chariot drawn by lions, shown with her son/lover Atis, who is wearing a Phrygian cap and breeches. The altar dates from the Roman period, when the cult of Cybele enjoyed a revival along with other mystery religions.

DAEDALUS

A genius craftsman of the classical world who could turn his hand and mind to almost anything. It was said that he was the only one who could create a golden honeycomb in openwork gold, apparently using a honeycomb and the lost wax (*cire perdue*) method. He was related to the royal house of Athens but was exiled for the crime of killing his nephew, Talos, in a fit of jealousy because of the talent he showed.

Daedalus went to Crete where he found employment with MINOS, the king. It was Daedalus who constructed a cow in which PASIPHAE, Minos' queen, could conceal herself and gratify her passion for her husband's prize bull. The outcome of this liaison was the MINOTAUR, half bull and half man, which Daedalus then had to conceal in the famous Labryinth, of which he was the architect. Either for assisting Pasiphae, or for helping THESEUS by suggesting to ARIADNE the ball of string trick, Minos imprisoned both Daedalus and his son ICARUS (whose mother was a palace slave, Naucrate). They managed to escape by means of large artificial wings which Daedalus constructed for them both and which were held together with wax. Daedalus reached Cumae safely, where he built a temple to Apollo before flying on to Sicily; Icarus flew too near the sun and the wax in his wings melted and he crashed into the sea and drowned.

In Sicily, Daedalus was well received by King Cocalus but the legends vary about his end. Some say that Cocalus killed him because of his fear of retribution from Minos; others that the daughters of Cocalus killed Minos when he came hunting Daedalus, and that Daedalus expressed his gratitude for the protection by designing many buildings for Cocalus.

DANAE

In Greek myth the daughter of Acrisius, king of Argos, and Eurydice. An oracle had told her father that his grandson would kill him. To prevent his daughter conceiving, Acrisius had Danae heavily guarded in an underground room of bronze into which no one was allowed, nor was she allowed out. It was all to no avail; Danae was seduced by ZEUS in the form of a shower of gold. In fury, when the boy PERSEUS was born Acrisius had mother and child cast into the sea in a wooden chest, hoping that the elements would perform the deed he could not do himself. They were cast up on the shore of the island of Seriphos and wel-

comed by Dictys, brother of the local king Polydectes. The latter fell in love with Danae but feared Perseus, so he sent him off to seek the head of the GORGON. Upon Perseus' successful return he and Danae returned to Argos, where he fulfilled the oracle by accidentally killing his grandfather Acrisius with a discus.

DAPHNE

A Greek river nymph, one of the many loves of APOLLO. He pursued the girl but, just as she was about to be caught, she called out to her father, the river Ladon (sometimes also said to be the river Pheneus), to save her. He or the gods heard, and transformed her into a laurel tree. Apollo made a wreath of laurel from its leaves for his head and decreed that the tree should henceforward be sacred to him.

Far left Dionysus, Greek God of wine, as portrayed on a Greek amphora of the fifth century BC, complete with his crown of vine leaves and leopard skin cloak.

Above Roman wall painting from Herculaneum of the first century AD, showing Daedalus with the Cretan queen Pasiphae. She points out to him the bull for which, inspired by Poseidon who wants vengeance on her husband Minos, she has developed an unnatural passion.

DEIANIRA

In Greek myth the daughter of Oeneus, king of Calydon, and Althea. She became the wife of HERACLES after he had gone down to Hades in search of CERBERUS; her brother MELEAGER met Heracles in Hades and asked him to marry his sister and look after her. This he did and they had a son, Hyllus. Once, when the couple were traveling together, they came to a swollen mountain stream and the centaur Nessus offered to carry Deianira across on his back. Heracles agreed, but when Nessus reached the opposite bank he tried to rape her. Heracles fired one of his magic poisoned arrows at the centaur and he fell dying. As he died, he gave his red-dyed tunic to Deianira, telling her that it would win back her husband's love if ever he should be tempted away.

In later years Heracles fell in love with Iole, whom he won as a prize in an archery competition arranged by her father, Eurytus. Deianira therefore sent him the centaur's tunic as a gift, to win him back, but when Heracles put it on the tunic began to burn his skin and he could not take it off. In agony, Heracles threw himself on to a funeral pyre on Mount Oeta. Deianira realized that the centaur had tricked her and committed suicide in her grief.

DEMETER

Sister of the Greek god ZEUS and one of the six children of CRONUS and RHEA, Demeter was the essential mother or fertility goddess and had many legends associated with her. She has very close parallels with the other major mother goddess figures of the earlier religions of the Near East, but principally with ISIS (except that Demeter produced a daughter, PERSEPHONE, and Isis a son, HORUS). Persephone's father was ZEUS, Demeter's brother, who was married to HERA. Mother and daughter are inextricably mixed in the legends. HADES (PLUTO) kidnapped Persephone, taking her down to his underground kingdom of the dead to rule there as his consort. Disconsolate, Demeter searched everywhere for her lost daughter, caring nothing for the earth or its crops and harvests. Eventually Helios, the sun god who sees everything, told her what had happened. Demeter vowed that she would not return to the gods or continue her fertility functions unless her daughter was returned to her.

During her absence the earth was barren and she took work as the wet-nurse for Triptolemus, the infant son of Celeus, King of Eleusis, and his wife Metanira. Demeter doted on the child and tried to make him immortal but his mother inter-

Below left This magisterial statue of Demeter the mother goddess comes from the Greek island of Knidos. Unusually among Greek deities, Demeter is quite often portrayed seated.

Below right Greek relief from the sanctuary of Demeter at Eleusis showing Demeter giving corn to Triptolemus, son of the king of Eleusis, whom Demeter nursed during the absence of her daughter Persephone in Hades.

Left A more static and archaic representation of Demeter between two warriors, still holding her ear of corn, symbol of fertility; from an Etruscan tomb painting.

vened (just as happened with Isis and the king of Byblos' son). When at last she discovered her daughter's abductor, Demeter went to Zeus and demanded her return from the Underworld. Zeus agreed, so long as Persephone had not eaten anything while she was there. All seemed to be well until it was found she had eaten some pips of a pomegranate. Zeus could not therefore keep his promise and Demeter withdrew her support of the earth and mankind – deadlock had been reached. Demeter did at least instruct the young Triptolemus in agriculture and gave him corn to take to mankind, but the fields still needed their fertility. Eventually a compromise was reached. Demeter would return to Olympia and Persephone would be let out from Hades at springtime when the earth received new vigor, but she had to return later in the year, at harvest-time and when winter approached, reflecting the annual cycle of decay and rebirth.

Demeter's greatest sanctuary was at Eleusis just outside Athens. Here the people of Attica came to thank and worship the goddess in the great Eleusian Mysteries. A large cave entrance is still pointed out there as one of the entrances to Hades' Kingdom of the Underworld.

Right Diana of Ephesus; this extraordinary many-breasted statue of the Roman goddess Diana was found in the forum at Ephesus, western Turkey, and is more in the tradition of the cult of Cybele, the Syrian mother goddess, than that of the virgin huntress.

DEUCALION DIANA

The Greek equivalent of the Biblical Noah and Mesopotamian UPNAPISHTIM. His father was PROMETHEUS and his mother Clymene, daughter of Oceanus. His wife was Pyrrha, the daughter of Epimetheus, a Titan, and PANDORA. ZEUS became angry at the vices and irreligious attitudes of mankind and decided to punish the human race, saving the only two decent people, Deucalion and Pyrrha. He therefore sent a great flood to devastate the earth, but Prometheus had advised Deucalion to build a large chest, an 'ark', and save himself and his wife in it. It floated on the flood waters for nine days and nights and finally came to rest on the mountains of Thessaly. Zeus then sent his messenger HERMES to them and offered to grant one wish. Deucalion's wish was that they should have some companions. Zeus granted this, but told them the way to effect it was to throw their mother's bones over their shoulders. Pyrrha was horrified at this and could not understand it but Deucalion realized that Zeus meant stones, the 'bones' of Mother Earth. This they did and as they walked along, tossing the stones over their shoulders, men sprang up from those that Deucalion threw and women from Pyrrha's stones. Deucalion then became king of Thessaly.

The Roman equivalent of the Greek ARTEMIS. In the Roman pantheon her parents were JUPITER and Latona whilst in Greek mythology they were ZEUS and LETO. She was the twin sister of APOLLO, born on the sacred island of Delos. In her Roman aspect, Diana was also the goddess of hunting and she had two particular shrines in Italy: one at Aricia on the shores of Lake Nemi, where she is known as Diana Nemorensis (Diana of the Woods), and the other at Capua under the name of Diana Tifatina (where she is the goddess of the crossroads and often associated with Hecate). In the eastern Empire her major shrine was at Ephesus, the temple of Artemis (one of the Seven Wonders of the Ancient World) and the location of the well-known biblical reference where the mob shouted 'Great is Diana of the Ephesians' against St Paul's teachings (Acts 19, 34). At Ephesus Diana was represented with a great many breasts and other symbols linking her with CYBELE.

The cult of Diana at Nemi, where she is often associated with Taurian Artemis, welcomed human sacrifices and her priest, known as the *Rex Nemorensis*, could be replaced by whoever killed him (this forms a core element of Sir James Frazer's great study *The Golden Bough*).

Left Diana appears in her more familiar guise, as the lithe and seductive but chaste huntress, in this second century AD mosaic from Tunisia.

DIDO

Queen of Carthage and one of the tragic figures of classical mythology, best known from the account in Virgil's *Aeneid*. Her origins lie much earlier in Phoenician legend, where she is Elissa, daughter of Mutto, king of Tyre, and sister of Pygmalion. Her brother Pygmalion inherited the kingdom but had Elissa's (Dido's) husband Sicharbas (the priest of Heracles) killed so that he could seize his wealth. Dido fled from Tyre with her adherents and, after making landfall in Cyprus, went on to North Africa, to Utica. Here she was well received and when she asked for land on which she and her party could settle, she was granted as much as could be covered by a bull's hide. She cut the hide into one very long, thin strip with which she was able to enclose a large tract of land outside Carthage, now known as the Hill of Byrsa. Recent excavations have shown that this area has the earliest evidence of settlement. It was from the nucleus of Byrsa that the later Carthage grew and spread.

Two versions are given of Dido's death. The local king, Iarbas, wished to marry her but she had no liking for the match. In order to gain time, she said that she needed three months to placate the spirit of her murdered husband Sicharbas. At the end of the time she had a great funeral pyre built and committed suicide on it. The other story tells of AENEAS arriving at Carthage and being welcomed by the Queen. When out hunting one day, they were overtaken by a storm and sought shelter in a cave where their love blossomed, a scene often depicted in Roman art. Iarbas called upon ZEUS to remove the stranger who stood in his way and Zeus, knowing that Aeneas was destined to found Rome, had him leave without even saying farewell to Dido. Learning that she had been abandoned, Dido committed suicide on a funeral pyre.

Right The sad story of Dido and Aeneas as portrayed in a mosaic which decorated the baths at a villa in Somerset, England – a surprising choice of subject for such a far-flung region of the Roman Empire. Successive scenes show Aeneas arriving with his fleet, being received by the queen of Carthage, going hunting with her, enjoying an idyllic love scene – and finally, in the central roundel, the abandoned Dido, eyes laden with grief, supported by two mourning Cupids.

DIOMEDES

There are two characters by this name in Greek legend, one a hero of the Trojan War and one an unpleasant king of Thrace.

The hero of Troy was the son of Tydeus and Deipyle. His early history is very involved but his major appearance is at Troy. There he was the constant companion of ODYSSEUS in all his exploits. Together they sought and found ACHILLES among the daughter of Lycomedes, persuaded AGAMEMNON to sacrifice IPHIGENIA for a favorable wind, stole the Palladium from the temple of Athena in Troy and ambushed and killed the spy

Dolan. He was a brave fighter who stood against both HECTOR and AENEAS, and also wounded ARES and APHRODITE when they became involved in the conflict.

It was said that Diomedes had one of the swiftest journeys back from the Trojan War, but when he got back to Argos he found that his wife Aegiale had been unfaithful to him (brought about by Aphrodite's malice at his having wounded her). She, rather like CLYTEMNESTRA, had plans to kill him but he escaped and left Argos, making his way to southern Italy. There his prowess earned him the daughter of king Danus in marriage but he later seems to have been killed by the king and his companions turned into birds in their grief at his death.

Left Diomedes and Heracles reveal Achilles in his disguise as one of the attendants of the daughter of King Lycomedes, as represented on a Roman wall painting from Pompeii of the first century AD. It had been foretold that Achilles would die if he accompanied the Greek expedition against Troy and, on the advice of his mother, the sea nymph Thetis, he hid at Lycomedes' court.

DIONYSUS

Greek equivalent to BACCHUS; although a late-comer to the ranks of the Twelve Olympian Gods, he had a huge and complex mythology built round him. Originally a wine god from Thrace, northern Greece, he soon found wide acceptance. He was the son of ZEUS by the nymph SEMELE. HERA, in her jealousy, brought about the death of Semele but Zeus was able to save the six-month-old unborn child to be born again from his thigh. To keep him out of harm's (Hera's) way, Dionysus was brought up by his aunt Ino and the nymphs of Nysa, but Hera learned of this and in vengeance sent Ino mad, while the nymphs became the constellation Hyades.

Dionysus met with many adventures as a young man. Lycurgus, king of Thrace, tried to take him prisoner but Dionysus escaped by hiding beneath the sea with the sea nymph Thetis. The king was driven mad and, imagining that he was attacking the vine, the sacred tree of Dionysus, he proceeded to hack at it with an ax. In his confused state he chopped off his son's hands and feet and cut his own leg. When he recovered his senses he realized that his kingdom had been struck sterile by the god. The only way that Dionysus could be appeased, and the curse lifted, was by the death of Lycurgus. His people had him torn apart by attaching a horse to each of his limbs and driving them off in different directions.

Pirates who kidnapped Dionysus for ransom, not knowing who he was, jumped overboard in terror when he manifested himself and turned the ship's mast into a sprouting vine; they were turned into dolphins.

A major part of his mythology is concerned with his journey to India, a semi-religious and military conquest. His triumphal return, accompanied by frenzied scenes, is often featured in art and especially on Roman sarcophagi. The Dionysiac or Bacchic rout is a major feature of his cult and involved women running riot in a religious

Right This magnificent dish made by the famous Greek potter Exekias in the mid-sixth century BC shows Dionysus, god of wine, sailing calmly across a charmed sea alive with dolphins, while the mast of his ship sprouts gladly into grape-laden vine stems.

Left This representation of Dionysus at his drunken revels, accompanied by a faithful leopard and a dancing maenad playing a tambourine, comes from a Roman funerary relief.

Left The Lycurgus cup, the finest surviving example of a figured cage-cup, shows the death of King Lycurgus, struggling in the grip of a predatory vine in retaliation for his impiety toward Dionysus.

73

ecstasy. The god revenged himself on Pentheus, king of Thebes, who was against the introduction of the cult of Dionysus, by having the king's wife, Agave, literally tear him apart in her religious frenzy.

Once Dionysus' cult was recognized world wide, he became a true god and was accepted amongst the Olympians. It was after this that he found ARIADNE asleep on Naxos and married her.

Music, dancing and revelry were his hallmarks, his instruments the cymbals and pipes and his emblem the *thyrsus*, a wine wand entwined in ivy. His adherents wore crowns of myrtle since legend said that he had given that plant, of which he was very fond, to Hades in exchange for releasing his mother Semele from the Underworld.

There are many fine representations relating to his cult and myth in ancient art, two notable examples being the fourth century AD carved Lycurgus Cup in the British Museum and the wall-paintings of a Dionysian/Bacchic ritual initiation in the House of the Mysteries at Pompeii.

DIOSCURI

The twin brothers Castor and Pollux were the sons of LEDA, wife of King Tyndareus of Sparta, by ZEUS. He visited her in the guise of a swan and her children, the twin boys and their sisters

Right This fourth century BC Etruscan bronze shows one of the Dioscuri, Castor or Pollux, with an equally athletic horse. Both twins were frequently represented with horses.

Left The Dioscuri carry off the oxen of their uncle Leucippos, in this limestone relief from Delphi.

HELEN and CLYTEMNESTRA, were born from an egg. The Dioscuri were involved in contests with THESEUS (who had carried off their sister Helen); they sailed with JASON and the ARGO-NAUTS and were present at the Calydonian Boar Hunt.

According to one legend, they abused the laws of guest hospitality when they were invited to the wedding feast of Lynceus and Idas, who were marrying the two daughters of Leucippus. Apparently the Dioscuri decided to carry off the two brides, and in the ensuing fight Castor was killed by Idas and Lynceus by Pollux. Zeus forthwith killed Idas with a thunderbolt and carried the wounded Pollux up to heaven. The brothers did not wish to be parted, Castor in Hades and Pollux in heaven, so Zeus allowed them to spend alternate days with the gods. Both were represented with horses, although Castor was the one skilled as a horseman and Pollux noted as a boxer. They subsequently became the constellation known as Gemini or The Twins. Because they had achieved divine status by the outbreak of the Trojan War, they were not involved, as one would expect, in the recovery of their sister Helen from PARIS at Troy.

In Roman legend the Dioscuri fought on the Roman side at the battle of Lake Regillus against the Latins in 496 BC. After the battle they were seen watering their horses at the Spring of Juturna in the Roman Forum to announce their victory. A temple to them is located nearby.

DUMUZI

Important Sumerian shepherd god, whose name is better known by the Hebrew form TAMMUZ, adopted as the name of the fourth month in the late Babylonian calendar, and still used as a month name in Hebrew and Arabic. The sources present a complexity of traditions about Dumuzi, probably originally a historical individual (he is referred to in the *Sumerian King List*) who also merges with traditions about the god Amaushum-galanna. Sumerian poetic texts attest to Dumuzi as the lover and husband of Inanna (see ISHTAR), and in *Innana's Descent to the Netherworld* he is sacrificed by her so that she may escape the clutches of the subterranean constabulary and return to Uruk. Dumuzi's death through Inanna also features in the story *Dumuzi's Dream*; He was certainly a figure of fertility. The fertility of Sumer was encouraged under, for example, the kings of the Ur III and Isin dynasties in an annual sacred marriage ritual, in which the king enacted the role of Dumuzi and the high priestess that of Inanna. There is no evidence that Dumuzi was a vegetation god, and earlier attempts to see in him the forerunner of J.G. Frazer's 'Dying God' who 'annually died and rose again from the dead', representing the 'yearly decay and revival of life, especially of vegetable life', are not at all borne out by cuneiform evidence.

EA

Sumerian Enki, Lord of the Earth or Underworld, the third most important god of the earlier Sumerian pantheon. He is the god of wisdom and magic, Lord of the Apsu, the cosmic sweet waters under the earth. Son of An, and brother to ADAD, he is father of ADAPA and Asalluhi (see MARDUK), who appears with him in many incantations against evil. Marduk notices the symptoms in a patient and goes to tell his father what has happened. Ea invariably replies, 'My son, what do you not already know? What can I add to you?' leaving Marduk to come up with a treatment from his own knowledge. His principal cult was located in the city of Eridu, where his temple was called Eabzu. Enki/Ea appears commonly in Mesopotamian myths, especially in Sumerian, where he is always a good friend to mankind, but often unreliable and mischievous in his behavior to other gods. His symbol is a turtle.

ECHO

There are two characters of this name in classical mythology, both nymphs. One was unsuccessfully wooed by PAN and then torn to pieces by local shepherds, only her voice surviving. The other, and better known, was a daughter of the Air and the earth goddess Tellus, and an attendant on HERA. She was deprived of speech by Hera because her chatter prevented the goddess catching her husband ZEUS in his amours with other nymphs; all poor Echo could do was repeat the last words spoken to her. She tried to make love to NARCISSUS with fragments of his own speech and, when he repulsed her, wasted away, only her voice remaining.

ELECTRA

Daughter of the Greek King AGAMEMNON and CLYTEMNESTRA, a major figure in Greek tragedy and prominent in the ORESTES cycle. There are several others of that name in mythology, but she is pre-eminent. After Agamemnon's return from Troy and his murder by Aegisthus and Clytemnestra, Electra was herself only saved by the intercession of her mother and then reduced to a servile condition, possibly even imprisoned in Mycenae. She saved her infant brother Orestes by smuggling him away to Strophus at Delphia where he was brought up with Pylades, the son of the house, thus beginning their life long friendship.

When her brother returned grown up, she recognized him at Agamemnon's tomb and incited him to kill their father's murderers. When he was subsequently pursued by the Erinyes (the FURIES) for the double murder and matricide, she stood by him. Orestes gave her in marriage to his friend Pylades who took her back to Phocis and they had two children, Medon and Strophius.

Far left This wonderfully decorated black-figure vase by the sixth century Greek master Exekias shows a marriage procession. Women are identifiable by their white-painted skin.

Below In this impression from a Babylonian cylinder seal, Ea, god of the deep, steps over a bull and out of the flowing water toward the sun god, who rises between two mountains. The goddess Ishtar stands on the right.

ENKIDU

In the Akkadian GILGAMESH Epic Enkidu is the wild man of the beasts who, defeated by Gilgamesh, becomes his firm friend and companion. In the earlier Sumerian Gilgamesh poems Enkidu's status is, by contrast, that of a servant.

ENLIL

Lord Wind, one of the principal gods of the Mesopotamian pantheon, worshiped especially in his temple Ekur in the city of Nippur. His parentage is variously given as Anu, chief of the gods, or the primal gods Enki and Ninki (different from EA/Enki). Many of the more important gods are described as his offspring, including ISHTAR/Inanna, Sin/Nanna-Su'en, NERGAL, NINURTA. Ningirsu (his prime son) and SHEMASH/Utu. His wife is usually Ninlil, although the grain goddess Sud has this status in some contexts. He is praised above all as cosmic administrator and the power in the storm. In some mythological passages he is a creative, benevolent god, but in the myth *Enlil and Ninlil* he rapes the young Ninlil, thus begetting Nanna-Su'en, and is banished from Nippur to the Underworld as a sex criminal. He is followed

by Ninlil and takes the form of three different men they meet on the journey to lie with her again, each time engendering another Underworld deity. In the cuneiform Flood stories it is Enlil who takes the decision to destroy mankind.

ENKI see EA

EPONA

Celtic horse goddess widely worshiped in Gaul, whose cult was introduced into Britain in Roman times. Regarded also as the Great Mother (*Magna Mater*), she is generally shown riding side saddle on a horse (cf ISIS in a similar position riding the dog star Sirius). When shown seated or standing she invariably has horses beside her. The horse was very important in Celtic mythology and much represented, as on the coins deriving from the gold staters of Philip II and also in the great hill figures such as the White Horse of Uffington. Epona was, without doubt, connected with the latter. As a mother goddess she is shown with *paterae* (dishes) of fruits and *cornucopiae* (horns of plenty). Some indication of her importance can be gathered from the fact that there are over 300 monuments to Epona known in Gaul. Her cult was particularly favored by Roman cavalry units along the Rhine and Danube frontiers, and in Britain all the epigraphic dedications to her occur in the area of Hadrian's Wall, again emphasizing her military connections.

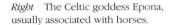

Right The Celtic goddess Epona, usually associated with horses.

Below On this bronze plaque from Hungary the horse goddess Epona is represented with a nameless warrior god, in Romanized form.

EROS

The Greek god of love (his Roman equivalent being CUPID), usually represented as a small chubby winged child, and the son of APHRODITE by either ZEUS, ARES or HERMES. There are numerous contradictions in the early legends and it is only later, mainly because of poetic writings, that he settles into the well-known form described. His attributes were a bow and a quiver full of arrows, the latter used to inflame love, as was the lighted torch he is sometimes shown wielding. He was always getting into scrapes but was benevolently tolerated by the gods. He could be shown playing – throwing a quoit, driving a hoop – or as a conqueror, with helmet on head and spear on shoulder. His power over both gods and men was indicated by showing him riding on a lion or dolphin, or breaking the thunderbolts of Zeus.

Above This charming bronze statue of a sleeping Eros dates from the late Greek or Hellenistic period.

Left A far more sensual and abandoned representation of Eros with Psyche, by the eighteenth century French sculptor Claude Michel, called Clodion.

Right A romantic eighteenth century view of Europa's abduction by Zeus disguised as a bull; this painting is by the German artist Jakob Frey.

ETANA

Below This Roman mosaic from southern France shows the abduction of Europa in an altogether milder and more mannered light.

Hero of the *Etana* myth, and a king of the First Dynasty of Kish, according to the *Sumerian King List*, ruling in the early third millennium BC. The

myth as now recovered tells of Etana's wife being childless and dreaming of the 'plant of birth', which her husband resolves to find for her. In the next scene there is a tree beside a river where an eagle and a serpent live harmoniously together as hunting partners. The eagle however, treacherously consumes the serpent's young, so the serpent goes weeping to Shamash for help. The latter shows him a trick to get the eagle caught in a pit. Etana rescues the eagle who transports him up to heaven on his back, in a famous episode that appears to be one the few mythological passages convincingly recognized in the art of cylinder seals. In fact there seem to be several flights involved, and a sequence of dreams, but the outcome of the myth seems to be that Etana and his wife do get a son.

EUROPA

The daughter of Agenor, King of Phoenicia, and Telephassa. Her famous brother was CADMUS. She was a beautiful girl who caught the eye of ZEUS one day while on the shore at Sidon (or Tyre). He transformed himself into a snow-white bull with crescent horns among the herds of Agenor and lay down at her feet as she gathered flowers in the meadows with her attendants. Her initial fear being overcome, she stroked the

EURYDICE

animal and then climbed upon its back. Immediately the bull headed for the sea and plunged in, making for Crete. Zeus took Europa to Gortyna in central Crete and there made love to her beneath a tree. This became part of the folklore of the area, even to the extent of a young girl in the branches of a tree being represented on the city's later coinage. Europa gave birth to three sons, MINOS, Sarpedon (who became king of Lycia and was killed at Troy by PATROCLUS), and Rhadamanthys (a just king who became one of the judges in Hades). From Zeus, Europa received three presents: the bronze man Talos who guarded the shores of Crete; a hunting spear that could never miss; and a dog that always ran its quarry down. Zeus then gave her in marriage to Asterion, king of Crete and, since the marriage was childless, he adopted Europa's three sons.

The subject of Europa and the Bull is a favorite one in classical and later European art. The bull subsequently became Taurus among the signs of the Zodiac and Europa gave her name to the continent of Europe.

In Greek myth the wife of ORPHEUS. While fleeing the unwelcome attentions of Aristaeus, a son of APOLLO, she was bitten by a snake and died. The gods were angry with Aristaeus and destroyed all his bees. In atonement to the shade of Eurydice he sacrificed four bulls and four heifers, leaving their carcases out to rot, at which swarms of bees returned to his land. Orpheus, however, in grief for his loss, made his way into the Underworld and succeeded in charming HADES with the music of his lyre to agree to release Eurydice. There was one condition: her shade would follow him to the upper air as he played, but he must not look back until he had reached daylight. Almost there, he could not resist the temptation to glance behind and see if she really was following. Immediately the condition was broken and she was dragged back into the Underworld.

Left Fourth century BC Greek relief showing Orpheus turning to look back at Eurydice as he leads her out of Hades. Hermes, leader of human souls, is shown preparing to take her back down into the Underworld. The Greek names above the figures are a modern addition and are incorrect.

FATES see ATROPOS, CLOTHO, LACHESIS

FENRIR

In Norse legend the monstrous wolf said to be the son of LOKI. He lived in Asgard, the home of the gods, but grew so large and fierce that he terrified the gods. Only one, TYR, dared to feed the beast; his jaws were so huge when open that they stretched from heaven to earth. The gods realized that the time had come for the wolf to be fettered for their safety, but no fetters they laid on him would hold. At last ODIN's wisdom devised an answer; the skilful dwarfs made him a chain from all the intangible elements, a fish's breath, a mountain's roots, the stealth of a moving cat, etc. No force could break this chain although it seemed little more than a silk cord. The gods again tried to fetter Fenrir but although the chain appeared simple and slight enough, he had his suspicions. He only agreed to the gods wrapping the chain round him if one of them would put his hand into his mouth as a gesture of good faith. No one wanted to do that, but in the end Tyr agreed. Fenrir was bound, struggled against the gossamer-thin chain and could not release himself and so he snapped his jaws shut. The gods were relieved that at last he was bound but Tyr lost his hand.

FREYA

(Frigg) in Norse legend the sister of FREYR and daughter of Njord. She was a very important goddess of fertility in the Northlands, the equivalent of the Great Mother goddesses of the Mediterranean area such as ISHTAR, ISIS, CYBELE, etc. Freya was recognized as the most beautiful of the northern goddesses and was married to ODIN (Woden). Her fertility aspect is emphasized in a number of the Icelandic Sagas by the various accusations of incest and promiscuity that are leveled at her. LOKI especially is prominent with

such calumnies. On the former count, brother/sister liaisons are commonplace in such fertility cults and ritual marriage was almost certainly a substantial part of her cult.

One of her particular attributes was her necklace, Brisingamen – a late account in the myths suggests that she earned it by accomodating for a night each of the four dwarfs who made it. Once again, there are parallels with ancient Near Eastern cults, notably in the prominence given to the goddess's necklace, which is so much a feature of many earlier statues and representations of the Great Mother. Freya was obviously closely involved in human love and the courtship and marriage rituals of the north, and was often called upon for assistance. The transference of her cult statue from place to place by means of a wagon is

Far left Romano-British deity.

Below Bronze statuette of the Viking period from Sweden, showing Freyr in his aspect of fertility god. He and his twin sister Freya were members of the Vanir, a group of Norse gods connected with growth and fertility.

Above This richly colorful and well preserved tapestry fragment from the twelfth century AD shows a Viking warrior on horseback. In remote areas of Scandinavia worship of the pagan Norse gods continued well into the second millennium.

often cited in the Sagas; sometimes there was no need for a statue to be in the covering wagon for the accompanying priest to announce the goddess's presence. The gift of prophecy was associated with Freya's cult image in the wagon, the 'answers' being translated by acolytes in attendance.

Freya also had another aspect more closely associated with her husband Odin and death. One Saga says that they divided the fallen heroes between them, taking bird form and swooping over the corpses on the battlefield.

Of all the female goddesses of the north, Freya, as would be appropriate for a fertility goddess, seems to have survived the longest. In the twelfth century AD the Icelandic chronicler Snorri Sturluson says that she still lived, i.e. was still the subject of worship in remote areas. The high incidence of her name incorporated into place names in Sweden and Norway certainly seems to bear out the idea of the late continuance of her cult in some form.

FREYR

The son of Njord, a Norse god connected with the sea and ships and the twin brother of the goddess FREYA; they were all part of a group of gods connected with fertility called the VANIR. Freyr is another of the Norse gods whose cult has much in common with some of those of the ancient Near East. His worship is closely connected with the idea of the divine marriage, in this instance with a young maiden Gerd, who lived in the Underworld with the giants. One day while sitting in ODIN's seat, Freyr saw Gerd at a distance and fell madly in love with her, so much so that he sent his servant and lifelong friend Skirnir with a horse for the perilous journey and gave him his (Freyr's) own magic sword that could fight of itself if he would woo Gerd on his behalf. At first the lady was reluctant and refused the gifts of the eleven golden apples and also of Odin's magic ring Draupnir. It was only when Skirnir, in desperation, cursed her with sterility that she agreed to meet and marry the lovesick Freyr nine nights later.

It was because he had given his sword to Skirnir that Freyr was consequently without a sword when the gods fought their last great battle, Ragnarok. There he was attacked and killed by Surtr, a fire giant, although the Ynglinga Saga has him die in his bed. Freyr, like BALDER, can be interpreted as the Young God who must die for the good of Mankind.

The cult of Freyr appears to have been based on his travelling around from place to place in a wagon, possibly similar to that found in the great Oseberg ship burial. Likewise, his sister Freya's cult involved a wagon and a priest who could tell when the goddess was present in it.

FURIES

In Greek legend three goddesses who inflict the vengeance of the gods on those who wrongly shed blood. They are also called the Erinyes, which literally means 'the angry ones', or Eumenides meaning 'the kindly ones', presumably in an attempt at appeasement. They were born from the drops of blood that flowed from the wound that SATURN inflicted on CRONUS and are envisaged as terrifying in appearance, wielding whips and torches and with serpents coiled in their hair. It is they who pursue ORESTES after he has killed his mother, despite the fact that he acted in obedience to APOLLO.

Left Greek bronze from the sixth century BC representing a Fury as a winged female figure, although in literary sources they are not usually described as winged.

GAIA

The archetypal mother in classical mythology, one of the earliest of the primitive gods from whom all the others sprang. She was born after Chaos in the primeval order and then, self-engendered, gave birth to URANUS (the sky), the Mountains, and Pontus (the sea). By Uranus she then bore six male and six female Titans, followed by the three Cyclops (one-eyed giants) and the three Hecatoncheires (violent, 100-armed creatures). Uranus became very tyrannical and so Gaia persuaded CRONUS, the youngest of the Titans who hated his father, to rid her of him. She gave him a sharp sickle and he castrated his father, throwing the testicles over his shoulder where the dripping blood resulted in Gaia giving birth to the three FURIES (the Erinyes), the Giants (huge beings with serpents instead of legs below their waist), and the Ash Nymphs.

Several of the early Greek poets, such as Hesiod, describe Gaia, although curiously she is not mentioned by Homer, where the gods concerned are all of the newer generation. Subsequently aspects of Gaia's role as Mother Earth were taken over by other goddesses such as CYBELE and DEMETER, to whom various of the gods were allocated as their offspring.

GANYMEDE

In Greek myth a very beautiful youth, a son of the Royal House of Troy. The legends vary as to who were his father and mother; generally, he was said to be the younger son of Tros and Callirhoe. ZEUS saw the boy and wished to have him on Mount Olympus. One day, while Ganymede was guarding his father's flocks close to Troy, Zeus flew down in the shape of an eagle and carried him off to Mount Olympus. There he acted as cupbearer and was specially employed to pour the nectar that Zeus drank. The story was a favorite one in ancient art and is often found on vessels to do with wine and also on mosaics; Ganymede, being lifted up by the eagle, can be found as far apart as the Roman villas at Bignor in Sussex and Paphos in Cyprus.

Far left Roman mosaic of the third century AD from Sousse in Tunisia, showing the beautiful Ganymede about to be carried off to Mount Olympus by Zeus, disguised as an eagle.

Below In this Roman relief the eagle Zeus drinks from the great wine dish held by Ganymede, who caresses him affectionately.

GEB

In Egyptian mythology the earth is envisaged as a god, contrasting with the Indo-European concept of the earth as a female principle. In the theogony of Heliopolis the offspring of ATUM, the god SHU and the goddess TEFNUT give birth to Geb the earth god and his sister-consort NUT, the sky goddess. Geb is often depicted supine, raising himself slightly on one arm and inclining the other upward towards the sky. His most crucial role is in the transmission of kingship. It is the children of Geb and Nut who form the link between the cosmic deities and the throne of Egypt – often referred to as the throne of Geb – namely OSIRIS, ISIS, SETH and NEPHTHYS. Geb was a presiding judge over HORUS and Seth, the disputants for the throne of Egypt following the murder of Osiris. His skin was shown as green, indicating the fruitfulness and fertility of the earth. It was thought that barley, a staple item of diet providing both bread and beer, grew from the ribs of Geb.

GILGAMESH

King of the city of Uruk, and hero of the *Epic of Gilgamesh*, which begins 'He who saw everything . . .', the most important literary composition to survive from ancient Mesopotamia. The epic is best known from the Akkadian (Standard Babylonian) version on twelve cuneiform tablets, dating to the seventh century BC, although a cycle of Sumerian stories (*Gilgamesh and Huwawa, Gilgamesh and the Bull of Heaven, Gilgamesh and Akka, Gilgamesh, Enkidu and the Netherworld* and *The Death of Gilgamesh*) shows that the material derives at least from the second millennium BC and quite probably from the third.

The Standard Babylonian epic which is here summarized is still incomplete, and the story is partly known from earlier sources. It begins by praising Gilgamesh, credited with composing the text himself, which was written on a stela and available in Uruk for all to read. Gilgamesh, two-thirds divine and one-third human, oppresses the young people of Uruk to the point that the goddess Aruru creates the wild man ENKIDU to challenge him. Enkidu, born and raised among wild animals, is the direct antithesis of Gilgamesh, and their clashing is inevitable. A trapper uses a harlot to seduce Enkidu, who has been freeing the animals caught in his traps, and thereby reduce his natural powers. Enkidu then challenges Gilgamesh, who defeats him in a wrestling match, after which the two become intimate friends.

In a later episode, to counter the softening effect of their settled existence, Gilgamesh proposes a dangerous expedition to the Cedar Forest, to defeat the formidable guardian HUMBABA, long known by reputation and feared by the reluctant Enkidu, and to cut down the sacred Cedar Tree. Gilgamesh finally persuades him and the Uruk elders, and special weapons are made. On the six-day journey Gilgamesh enlists the help of SHAMASH, the sun god, and has a series of ominous dreams which are expounded by Enkidu. Tensions between the two lead to a fight but they persevere, and reach and enter the Cedar Forest. After a battle Humbaba is defeated with the assistance of Shamash, who sends fierce winds to dis-

Left Old Babylonian plaque showing a god or hero who may well represent Gilgamesh; it dates from about 2000 BC. The story of Gilgamesh with its many episodes is one of the principal strands in Babylonian mythology.

Right Marble Medusa head, standing more than ten feet high at the temple of Apollo, Didyma, in western Turkey. It was probably intended to ward off malign influences from the sanctuary.

Far right This archaic Greek Gorgon adorned the center of the pediment, or temple front, of the temple of Artemis in Corfu. Her winged sandals and snakes are more in keeping with the Gorgon's reputation than the calm face at Didyma.

tract Humbaba. He is despatched by a hesitant Gilgamesh, who keeps the head as a trophy. The heroes cut down the sacred Cedar and, building a raft from Humbaba's trees, sail back down the Euphrates to Uruk.

Once returned, Gilgamesh is beset with other problems. The goddess ISHTAR attempts to seduce and wed him, but he spurns her with a scornful reference to her ill-fated earlier lovers and she is roused to fury. She persuades her father Anu to send the Bull of Heaven against Uruk, regardless of consequences. Many of the population lose their lives in pits made by the Bull before Gilgamesh and Enkidu defeat it, and Gilgamesh kills it with his sword, then hurls its thigh in Ishtar's face. Enkidu then has a dream from which it emerges that his part in these feats requires punishment by death. Despite his protestations Enkidu succumbs after a decline of twelve days, accusing Gilgamesh of having abandoned him. Gilgamesh mourns his friend profoundly, ordering a statue to be made. Realizing in his grief that one day he too will have to die, Gilgamesh turns to the pursuit of eternal life. He determines to gain the secret from UTANAPISH-TIM, the only man to have achieved immortality for his part in saving life from the Flood. Gilgamesh starts on a journey to the Mouth of the Rivers to see him. The scorpion-man and his mate attempt to dissuade him from the journey, as does Siduri, the tavern-keeper, who points to the folly of his search in one of the most powerful and affecting passages in cuneiform. Gilgamesh finds Urshanabi, the Ferryman, who instructs him how to cross with safety the Waters of Death. Armed with punting poles they cross and Gilgamesh meets Utanapishtim. Once he has revealed the nature of his search Utanapishtim tells Gilgamesh the full story of the Flood, and how he rescued his family and all the beasts and animals of the field. This, the eleventh tablet of the series, has provided the closest parallel to the flood narrative in *Genesis*. After further difficulties Gilgamesh is shown how to gain the Plant of Eternal Youth, but while he bathes in a spring a snake steals and eats it, immediately sloughing its old skin. Gilgamesh then resolves to return empty-handed to Uruk. It is often considered that this point marks the end of the original narrative but the Standard Edition contains a twelfth tablet, in which Enkidu goes down into the Underworld to rescue two objects that have been lost there and is trapped there. Gilgamesh summons his ghost to ask about conditions in the land beyond the grave. This tablet is a direct translation from the Sumerian *Gilgamesh, Enkidu and the Netherworld* and is regarded by many as an artifical appendage to the eleven-tablet series.

GUNNAR

Norse hero who marries the Valkyrie BRUN-HILDA with the assistance of SIGURD.

Below The three Graces, although they figure in classical mythology, appear more frequently in Renaissance than in classical art, as the epitome of the ideal female. This roundel dates from 1525.

GORGONS

These were three sisters, Stheno, Eurale and MEDUSA, who were the daughters of the sea gods Phorcys and Ceto. The first two of the sisters were immortal but the third, Medusa, was mortal and she is the one who is best known and most often referred to as the Gorgon, as if there was only one. The sisters lived in the far west, close by the Kingdom of the Dead. They were of frightful aspect with snakes entwined in their hair, hands of brass (or bronze), teeth as long as boars' tusks, bodies covered with impenetrable scales and wings of gold. Their glance was so terrible that it turned the beholder to stone. Only POSEIDON, of all the gods and men, was not afraid of them, and he fathered the giant Chrysaor and the winged horse PEGASUS on Medusa. It was the hero PERSEUS who finally killed her.

HAPY

HADES

The god of the dead in classical mythology, known to the Romans as PLUTO. Unlike similar deities in other religions, e.g. OSIRIS in Egypt, he was seen as a pitiless and frightening god. Hades was the son of CRONUS and RHEA and therefore the brother of ZEUS. In the great division of the world after the defeat of the Titans, Hades was given Hell, or Tartarus, as his share while Zeus took the earth and heavens and POSEIDON the sea.

Hades wanted a wife and he cast his eyes on PERSEPHONE, his niece, the young daughter of Zeus and DEMETER. Her parents would have none of the match (although Zeus appears to have connived at subsequent events). Hades therefore took matters into his own hands and kidnaped the girl one day while she was out picking flowers with other young girls in the plains of Sicily, and took her down into the Underworld. The gods were angry and Demeter mourned her daughter, causing the earth to be barren, i.e. winter. Hades was told to restore the girl to her mother, but he had foreseen this and had given Persephone the seed of a pomegranate to eat. Anyone who had eaten anything in the Underworld could not re-

turn to the earth to live. A compromise was reached; Persephone would spend a third of the year in the Underworld as Hades' wife, but she could return to earth the rest of the time. Demeter was satisfied with this, and Persephone, upon her return each year from below ground, personified the Spring, renewal, just as the flowers and seeds pushed their way up through the earth at that season.

HAPY

Personification in Egyptian mythology of the phenomenon of the Nile flood, one that has vanished from modern Egypt. In pharaonic Egypt the increase in the volume and speed of the river, beginning about the end of July, was eagerly awaited – the fields would be freshened and a new layer of fertile silt carried all the way from Ethiopia would be the basis of a rich harvest. Hapy lived in the caverns in the vicinity of the cataract and possessed an androgynous body – pendulous breasts and swollen paunch – to indicate the fecundity brought to Egypt by the flood. His crown was often a clump of papyrus which grew prolifically by the river Nile.

Far left This restored Greek sculpture demonstrates the terrible fate that could befall those who offended Hera, queen of the Greek gods. Laocoon was high priest in the temple of Apollo at Troy; he advised the Trojans against allowing in to Troy the Wooden Horse left by the ingenious Greeks on the plain outside the city. Hera, however, favored the Greek cause because she had not been chosen as the most beautiful goddess in the Judgment of Paris. She therefore sent two enormous serpents to devour Laocoon and his two sons; the Trojans, hailing this as a portent, hauled the horse within the walls, thus ensuring the destruction of Troy.

Left The harpies were winged monsters with the faces of women and the bodies of vultures. Originally creatures of plunder and destruction, they became associated with the passage of the dead soul to the Underworld. The Harpy Tomb at Xanthos in western Turkey, from which this detail is taken, shows them carrying off the bodies of the deceased.

93

HATHOR

In Egyptian mythology the goddess Hathor is a complex deity. As a cow goddess the aspect of the universal mother predominates but does not eclipse her role as symbolic consort of the pharaoh by virtue of being the wife of the hawk-god HORUS. There are three major forms under which Hathor, daughter of the sun god RE, can appear in Egyptian iconography. Firstly she can be depicted as an elegant woman wearing a crown of cow-horns with the sun disk between them. Secondly she can assume the total body of a cow, often in this form suckling the young monarch with her udder of divine milk. Thirdly in architectural elements her face is human but her ears are bovine. It was a natural step for Greeks to equate Hathor with APHRODITE. She was a goddess of sexual love, of joy, of music and of dance. Love poetry from Egypt abounds with allusions to her as the 'Golden One'. In the story of the struggle between Horus and SETH for the throne of Egypt, where the sun god Re, her father, goes off to sulk over a slight, it is Hathor who brings him back into the proceedings by going to him and displaying the intimate parts of her body.

Far left This head of the Egyptian goddess Hathor shows her with human face but bovine ears. In her aspect as a cow goddess she reflected the principle of the universal mother.

Left The Trojan hero Hector, son of Priam king of Troy, fights Menelaus for the body of Euphorbus, another Trojan warrior whom Menelaus has killed. This unusual plate was painted on the island of Rhodes.

HECTOR

Foremost of the Trojan warriors and the eldest son of PRIAM, king of Troy, and his wife Hecuba. He was married to Andromache, daughter of king Aetion of Thebes in Mysia (which town had been sacked by ACHILLES in the ninth year of the Trojan War, and Andromache's father and seven brothers killed). Hector and Andromache had a son called Astyanax.

In the *Iliad*, which is only concerned with the tenth and last year of the Trojan War, Hector plays a very prominent role. Whenever Achilles is not present on the Greek side, everything falls before Hector. AGAMEMNON had wanted Hector killed from the outset because he knew that the Greeks could never win while Hector lived. Many of Hector's exploits are noted in the legends and also often illustrated in Greek vase paintings, notably his day-long fight with Ajax, at the end of which both combatants retired and gave each other presents.

The attack on the Greek ships, planned and led by Hector, was perhaps his greatest exploit. The Greeks were hard pressed and Achilles refused to leave his tent where he was sulking. PATROCLUS, Achilles' close friend, in an endeavor to turn the tide, donned Achilles' armour and fought but was

killed by Hector. This at last brought Achilles to his senses and he emerged into the fray seeking revenge. Hector's destiny was to die at the hands of Achilles and so, no matter what the gods did to assist, for example once hiding him in a cloud from Achilles, his life could only be prolonged and not saved. The petty jealousies and favoritism of the gods played quite a part in this. ATHENA took the form of Hector's favourite brother, Delphobus, and urged him to stand against Achilles, promising to help him. Eventually Achilles and Hector met outside the Scaean Gate; Athena disappeared and Hector knew his fate was sealed. APOLLO and ARES, his supporters till then, also deserted him. Hector was struck down and, as he lay dying, he entreated Achilles to return his body to his father Priam but Achilles refused. Hector then foretold Achilles' own iminent death.

Achilles treated Hector's corpse abominably, piercing the heels and passing a leather thong through them and then dragging it around the walls of Troy in revenge for the death of Patroclus. The body was then left exposed in the Greek camp. Achilles refused all appeals for clemency or offer of ransom until the gods were so repelled by his actions that Zeus sent Iris to order him to release Hector's corpse for decent burial. For a large sum he ransomed the body to Priam, and subsequently Hector's twelve-day long funeral rites were performed under a truce.

Far left The goddess Hathor, seated in a sycamore tree, supplies a thirst-quenching drink of water to the deceased who, accompanied by the soul-bird Ba, is about to start on his journey through the Underworld.

Right This detail from the so-called Heimdall Cross Slab, found on the Isle of Man, shows Heimdall as warder of the gods sounding his horn to call them to Ragnarok, the last great battle in which the Norse world ends.

Below The Greek princess Helen is represented on this Greek krater or wine cooler with her Trojan abductor Paris, his brother Hector, and Hector's wife Andromache. Although at first perhaps reluctant, it seems that Helen soon became accustomed to her captivity and here looks very much the devoted wife.

HEIMDALL

A curious member among the pantheon of the Norse gods, Heimdall is said variously to be one of the sons of ODIN and also the son of nine maidens, all sisters, who gave him birth in common. He was the 'Guardian of Heaven', since he guarded the gate into Asgard, living beside the Bifrost Bridge at Heaven's Edge with his horse which was called Goldtopping. His duty was to keep watch, especially for the anticipated attack by the Giants.

Heimdall was also a benevolent fire god and, as such, was the antithesis of LOKI, the evil one who was his sworn enemy. He thwarted Loki on several occasions, principally when Loki stole FREYA's magic necklace Brisingamen. Loki left this on a rock in the middle of the sea and Heimdall, taking the form of a seal, swam out and retrieved it, fighting off Loki, and returned it to its rightful owner in Asgard.

Heimdall was the Watchman of the Gods, ready to summon them at the final battle of Ragnarok, the 'Doom of the Gods'. He is usually represented with the great horn that he sounded only in the direst emergency, to summon the gods to war. Like all the other inhabitants of Asgard, he perished at the battle of Ragnarok, destroyed by his counterpart Loki, the manifestation of fire as a malevolent force.

HELEN

Greek princess who has become the epitome of female beauty. She was the cause of the Trojan War ('the face that launched a thousand ships, and burnt the topless towers of Ilium' as Christopher Marlowe wrote). Helen's legend is extremely complicated, especially as recorded by ancient writers after Homer. She was the daughter of ZEUS by LEDA, whom he visited as a swan. Leda subsequently produced an egg from which were born Helen and her twin brothers the DIOSCURI Castor and Pollux. Her mortal sister (the daughter of Tyndareus and Leda) was CLYTEMNESTRA.

From an early age Helen's beauty attracted many suitors. She was carried off by THESEUS before the age of ten and rescued by her twin brothers. Tyndareus, her mortal father, was very concerned by the number of her suitors, given variously as from 29 to 99. He realized that whoever he chose as Helen's husband, he would offend the rest and conflict would follow. The wily ODYSSEUS suggested a clever solution: the suiters were all sworn to accept Helen's choice and to support him should the need ever arise. She chose MENELAUS, king of Sparta, and it was this oath that Menelaus invoked after her abduction by PARIS. Odysseus was rewarded with the hand in marriage of PENELOPE, Tyndareus' niece. Helen and Menelaus had a daughter, Hermione.

APHRODITE had promised Paris the most beautiful woman in the world if she was awarded the Apple of Discord in his judgment between herself, HERA and ATHENA. She won the contest and Paris, on a visit to the Spartan court, seduced Helen and took her, together with a vast treasure and Helen's slaves (but not her daughter Hermione) away to Troy. Menelaus invoked the oath and the support of the other princes and they sailed to besiege Troy.

Helen was looked upon as Paris' wife in Troy, but she was disliked by the Trojans who regarded her as the cause of their misfortunes. Only HECTOR and PRIAM realized that the will of the gods was being carried out and she was an innocent victim of that will. Although in sympathy with the Greeks, Helen, while in Troy, would stand on the walls and identify the Greek leaders for the Trojans; yet it was also said that she twice recognized Odysseus when he entered Troy in disguise and did not give him away. On the second occasion she apparently actively assisted him when he stole the Palladium along with DIOMEDES.

When Troy fell to the stratagem of the Wooden Horse, Helen took refuge in the sanctuary of Apollo, where her vengeful husband Menelaus found her and forgave her. Their return home to Sparta took eight years and, like that of Odysseus, was beset with misfortune. Various versions of her death are given. Homer said that she became the epitome of the virtuous wife and was subsequently deified (along with Menelaus her husband, apparently at her request to recompense him for all the wrongs she had done him). Another account has her enjoying eternal life with ACHILLES (her fourth husband in some legends) on an island in the Euxine Sea. Several variant stories have revenge as the theme of her death: she hung herself in remorse; she was offered in sacrifice in Tauris (cf IPHIGENIA), or she was killed by Thetis, Achilles' mother, for having been the indirect cause of his death. Five heroes are associated with her as 'husbands': Theseus, Menelaus, Paris, Achilles and, lastly, Deiphobus after Paris' death.

HEPHAESTUS

The smith god, son of ZEUS and HERA. He is always portrayed clad in a leather apron and as being lame. It was said that his lameness came about because he took his mother's (Hera's) part on Olympus in an argument with Zeus. In anger Zeus threw him from Olympus and he fell for a whole day before landing on the island of Lemnos, thus causing his deformity. Another version says that he was born deformed and Hera threw him into the sea in disgust. He lived in a cave on Lemnos for nine years and learnt the secrets of metalworking. Volcanoes were his workshops and his creations masterpieces. It was to Hephaestus that Thetis turned when she wanted the finest armor made for her son ACHILLES and he also forged Zeus's thunderbolts.

Zeus married Hephaestus to APHRODITE, but she was unfaithful to him with ARES. Helios the sun god saw the two lovers together one day and told Hephaestus. He made an invisible net which could not be broken and strung it about Aphrodite's bed. When she was with her lover he sprang the trap and then called all the gods to see the pair enmeshed in the net. When he released them, Aphrodite hid herself in shame.

Below The temple of Hephaestus overlooking the agora or market place in Athens is one of the most perfectly preserved of all classical temples. It faces across the agora to the Parthenon.

HERA

In Greek myth the long-suffering and at times spiteful wife of ZEUS, the daughter of CRONUS and RHEA and therefore also Zeus' sister. She was violently jealous of her husband's liaisons with various mistresses and often tried to bring about their harm, even death, or pursued their children. She caused the death of SEMELE, DIONYSUS' mother, and urged others to appalling deeds in her vindictiveness. At times she went too far and Zeus intervened, as when she endeavored to shipwreck HERACLES upon his return from Troy. Zeus had her hung by her wrists from Olympus with an anvil tied to each foot. She is also credited with having instigated Heracles' Twelve Labors as a punishment.

Several places are suggested where Zeus married Hera, including the Gardens of the Hesperides, but the pair are generally associated with Crete (where Zeus was brought up on Mount Ida) and with the area of Knossos (in commemoration of which Hera's head appears on some of the coins of Knossos). Zeus and Hera had four chil-

Above The Greek temple of Hera at Paestum in southern Italy was built in the mid-fifth century BC, its cigar-shaped columns typical of the contemporary building style.

Right Architectural sculpture from the temple at Selinunte, Sicily, showing the marriage of Zeus, overlord of the Greek gods, and Hera. The faces and arms are of Parian marble but the rest is carved in local limestone which has weathered badly.

Far right above This wonderfully animated scene from an archaic Greek vase of the sixth century BC shows the hero Heracles battling with the monster Geryon, one of the Twelve Labors imposed on him by the jealous Hera.

Far right below Graphic portrayal on a sixteenth century Italian earthenware dish of the birth of Heracles; the laboring Alcmena is shown in a wholly contemporary setting in the central roundel, surrounded by the seven virtues and planets.

dren: ARES, HEPHAESTUS, Eileithyia and Hebe (the last two respectively the goddesses of child-birth and youth).

The major sanctuary of Zeus was at Olympia (where his chryselephantine statue by Pheidias was one of the Seven Wonders of the Ancient World) and Hera also had a temple alongside it. Her major shrine, however, was located in the plain of Argos and known as the Argive Heraion. It had a famous cult statue of her by the sculptor Polycleitos.

It was again in revenge – because she had lost (along with ATHENA) the beauty contest judged by PARIS – that Hera sided with the Greeks in the Trojan War. She was the especial protectress of ACHILLES, more so since she had brought up his mother, Thetis.

HERACLES

In Roman legend Hercules, the greatest of the heroes in classical mythology. He was the son of ZEUS by a Theban girl Alcmena and his conception is supposed to have taken three days and three nights to accomplish. Zeus' wife HERA singled Heracles out from among Zeus' many progeny as the focus of her anger and resentment, sending two snakes to destroy him when he was a baby of eight months, which the infant hero easily strangled. In early manhood he destroyed the lion of Mount Cithaeron and delivered his country from an annual tribute of 100 oxen, but was driven mad by Hera and killed his own family in his frenzy. To expiate this crime the famous Twelve Labors were imposed on him by Eurystheus, king of Mycenae. These were: the killing of the Nemean lion, which he did with his bare hands, subsequently wearing the skin of the animal as a cloak; the destruction of the seven-headed hydra, a creature sacred to Hera; the capture of the Arcadian stag; the capture of the Erymanthian boar, a creature that frightened Eurystheus so much that he hid in a storage pot for several days, a scene often depicted in Greek vase painting; the cleaning of the Augean stables, where 3000 oxen had been kept for many years; the killing of the carnivorous Stymphalian birds; the capture of the bull which POSEIDON had sent to ravage Crete; the capture of the meat-eating mares of Diomedes; the stealing of the girdle of HIPPOLYTA, queen of the Amazons; the killing of the monster Geryon and the capture of his flocks; bringing apples from the garden of the Hesperides, who guarded the fruit that GAIA gave to Hera on her marriage to Zeus; and fetching the three-headed hound CERBERUS from the Underworld. He subsequently married DEIANIRA, who unwittingly brought about his death by giving him a poisoned tunic to wear. ·

HERMES

Right Hermes as the epitome of male beauty, created by the renowned Greek sculptor Praxiteles. The messenger god holds the infant Dionysus, god of wine.

In Greek mythology the messenger of the gods, son of ZEUS and the nymph Maia; his Roman equivalent is MERCURY. He also had the role of escorting the dead to the Underworld, and later became identified with the Norse god ODIN, in his aspect of father of the slain. Hermes was also the patron of merchants and seamen, of good luck, and of thieves and pickpockets, and was renowned for his mischief-making. On the day after his birth he stole the oxen of Admetus which APOLLO was guarding, and is credited with the invention of the lyre, which he gave the irate god as a peace-offering. Zeus often used him as an intermediary in his various amours, and gave him as a reward the winged helmet and sandals with which he is usually represented and which he lent to PERSEUS. In another aspect Hermes was god of roads and of fertility, as represented by wayside shrines or *hermeia*, which were quadrangular pillars with a bust of the god on top and a phallus carved below.

Right Hermes, wearing the winged helmet given him by Zeus, presides over the funeral rites of the Greek hero Sarpedon who, during the course of the Trojan war, killed so many Greeks that, when he was at last slain by Patroclus, he was given special funerary honors by order of Zeus.

HERYSHAF

In Egyptian mythology an ancient ram-god particularly worshiped at a site called Henes not too far from modern Berisuef in Middle Egypt. The identification of Heryshaf with HERACLES by the Greeks led to this cult centre and city becoming known as Herakleopolis. The symbolism inherent in the name Heryshaf, which means 'he who is upon his lake', is clearly that of a primeval deity emerging out of the watery chaos at the beginning of time. Heryshaf was envisaged as a universal sovereign 'King of the Two Lands'. Also he became a form of the sun god and the northern breeze of his nostrils adds the notion of a creator deity to the solar imagery.

HIPPOLYTA

Queen of the Amazons and a warrior maiden, who was given in marriage to THESEUS by HERACLES after he had conquered her and removed her girdle as one of his Twelve Labors. In another version Theseus falls in love with Hippolyta and throws down his sword in battle against her.

HIPPOLYTUS

Son of THESEUS and HIPPOLYTA. After the death of his mother Theseus married Phaedra, who fell in love with her stepson and tried to seduce him. He resisted her advances, so infuriating her that she accused him to Theseus of raping her. Theseus in anger asked POSEIDON to punish his son, and Poseidon sent a sea monster, which so terrified Hippolytus' horses as he fled in his chariot along the seashore that they bolted among the rocks and Hippolytus was killed.

HODER

The blind god of Norse mythology, the unfortunate scapegoat. He was a son of ODIN (his brothers/half-brothers are BALDER, HEIMDALL, Hermod, THOR, TYR, and Vali; like ZEUS, Odin fathered sons on various goddesses as well as FREYA his wife). Hoder was the weak link among

Above An Amazon warrior maiden in battle with a Greek, from the mausoleum at Halicarnassus, Turkey.

Left Richly decorated Egyptian pectoral showing Pharaoh smiting his enemies under the sheltering wings of the hawk god Horus.

the gods because it was through his blindness that LOKI was able to effect his evil designs on Balder. Hoder, his hand guided by Loki, brought about Balder's death, by flinging the deadly dart of mistletoe at him. Odin knew that this act would lead to the downfall of the gods, the Ragnarok; quarrelling would break out and Vali would avenge Balder by slaying Hoder.

HORATIUS

Legendary hero of ancient Rome who, together with two companions, defended the Sublician bridge across the River Tiber against the army of the Etruscans led by Lars Porsena, while the Romans destroyed the bridge so that the Etruscans could not cross. His two companions jumped to safety before the bridge fell, but Horatius remained on the far side and then jumped with all his weapons into the Tiber, commending his life to the god of the river, as Lord Macaulay described in his *Lays of Ancient Rome*:

Oh, Tiber! Father Tiber!
To whom the Romans pray,
A Roman's life, a Roman's arms,
Take thou in charge this day!

The river duly bore him up and delivered him safely on the Roman side, and Horatius was given as reward as much land as he could plow in a day.

HORUS

The Egyptian hawk-god Horus is exceptionally complicated to analyze since he is a deity of the distant sky in his solar aspect and yet immediate and present among the Egyptians is his manifestation of the pharaoh. The name Horus means 'the one far-off' or 'He on high'. Representations show Horus both wholly in the form of a hawk (as early as the late Predynastic Period just prior to 3000 BC) and human to the shoulders with the head of the hawk. The iconography of the hawk itself symbolized the sky with its wings and the sun and moon with its two eyes. An ubiquitous motif in Egyptian architecture and relief is that of a winged sun-disk. This too is Horus as 'He of Behdet' (a sanctuary in the north-east Delta) and announces without need of explanatory text that the hawk propels the sun-disk across the heavens. As Horakhte he subsumed under his identity the Great Sphinx at Giza, originally constructed in the image of the pharaoh Khafre (2520-2494 BC) as a human-headed lion guarding the causeway leading to the king's pyramid.

The other side to Horus is his role in the myth of the transmission of the throne of Egypt. His mother was the goddess ISIS who conceived him by her magical power from the body of his murdered father OSIRIS. His name Harsiese means just 'Horus Son of Isis'. When he reached maturity as Haroeris or 'Horus the Elder' he was able to make his bid for the throne of Egypt, occupied by the usurper SETH. The richest source of information on the struggle of Horus against Seth can be found in a racy, even scandalous, account surviving on a papyrus in the British Museum, written about 1150 BC. The opening scenes are set in a tribunal established to decide on the legality of the rival claims of Horus and Seth. Seth is supported by the sun god RE as being entitled to the throne by virtue of being the older. Horus and Seth engage in a series of contests to prove their claims. In one episode Seth feigns reconciliation with Horus but makes a homosexual attack on him. Horus foils it, without Seth realizing, and collects Seth's semen. Isis throws it into the marshes and spreads some of the semen of Horus himself on a bed of lettuces, Seth's favorite food, which Seth predicably eats. The result is that when Seth before the gods tries to humiliate Horus as a result of sexually assaulting him, his semen which he believed was in Horus is found to answer him from the marshes. In fact is is Seth who is humiliated because the semen of Horus emerges from his head. Another contest sees Horus and Seth change into hippopotami to ensure three months submergence under water.

Eventually the award of the kingship of Egypt is given to Horus, which means that the pharaoh, regarded as the living manifestation of the god, legitimately rules Egypt by virtue of the verdict of the divine tribunal. We are left in no doubt about the identification between the monarch and Horus when we admire the majestic diorite statue of Khafre in Cairo Museum where the hawk god spreads his wings protectively behind the royal headcloth. Finally the god permeates Egyptian iconography and funerary and temple inscriptions in the most powerful amuletic symbol known as the 'Wadjat Eye' or 'Eye of Horus'. In one episode of the contest for the throne Seth gouged out Horus's eyes leaving him vulnerable. HATHOR rubbed Horus with the milk of a gazelle which restored his sight. The imagery of the 'Sound Eye' ('Wadjat' in Egyptian) is a puissant sign of protection and perfection and takes the form of a human eye with a cosmetic line and eyebrow, with the feathered marking of a hawk's cheek below it.

HUMBABA

(Sumerian Huwawa), the guardian of the Cedar Forest appointed by ENLIL whom GILGAMESH and ENKIDU defeated together in the Gilgamesh Epic. It is clear from representations on cylindar seals depicting this scene that the terrifying Humbaba was human in body with lion's claws, distorted staring face and much hair. Clay models probably prepared for teaching purposes depict Humbaba's face, which is likened to a sheep's intestines.

Far left Statue of the hawk god Horus from the temple of Horus at Edfu, Egypt; he could be portrayed either wholly as a hawk wearing the god's tall crown, as here, or human to the shoulders with a hawk's head.

Above Egyptian stela of the fifth century BC showing Horus in wholly human form but with a hawk headdress, in a scene from his childhood when he vanquished the predatory crocodiles of the Nile.

Left Horus in human form with hawk's head in a fifteenth century BC wall painting from the temple of Hatshepsut, Luxor, Egypt.

Far left The Egyptian goddess Isis accompanies the mummified body of her murdered husband Osiris on its journey downriver, from the *Papyrus of Ani*, part of the Theban *Book of the Dead*. Osiris was killed through the machinations of the god Seth, and became ruler of the Egyptian Underworld.

Left Icarus hovers triumphantly on the wings which his father Daedalus made from wax and feathers in this wall painting from the Roman city of Pompeii. His triumph was shortlived, however; the sun melted the wax and Icarus was drowned in the sea.

ICARUS

In Greek myth the son of DAEDALUS who, with his father, fled from Crete on wings made of wax and feathers to escape the wrath of MINOS. Daedalus arrived safely in Attica but Icarus in his pride flew too close to the sun, which melted the wax in his wings so that he fell into the sea and was drowned.

IMDUGUD see ANZU

IMHOTEP

The most important example of an ancient Egyptian official gaining such fame and prestige that eventually he became deified. He is historically attested as the vizier of King Netjerykhet or Djoser (2630-2611 BC) for whom the Step Pyramid at Saq-

qara was built. Imhotep was the architect of this pyramid which was the first large scale stone monument ever constructed in the world. He was given the privilege of having his name and titles carved on the pedestal of a statue of the pharaoh. By the ptolemaic era Imhotep was deified and worshiped as a god from Saqqara to the temple of Isis at Philae. His reputation in medicine as a healer led to a natural identification between him and the Greek god ASCLEPIUS.

INANNA see ISHTAR

IO

In Greek myth a priestess of HERA at Argos. ZEUS fell in love with her and visited her disguised in cloud and mist. The jealous Hera surprised them together and, to save his mistress, Zeus changed her into a beautiful heifer. Hera then persuaded Zeus to give her the heifer as a gift and set the

Above Musicians and priests prepare for a sacrifice on this sixth century BC wooden panel from New Corinth. Here the sacrifice is a ram, but a similar scene would have greeted the unfortunate Iphigenia when she was summoned to Aulis by her father Agamemnon; only the intervention of the goddess Artemis saved her.

Right This terracotta figure from the Mesopotamian city of Ur shows Ishtar in her fertility aspect, with flowing hips and hands clasped on breasts.

hundred-eyed Argus to watch her, but Zeus sent HERMES to destroy Argus and release Io, still in heifer form. She reached Egypt, pursued by Hera's jealousy, where Zeus restored her human form and, in one version, she married OSIRIS and was worshipped under the name of ISIS.

IPHIGENIA

In Greek legend daughter of AGAMEMNON, high king of Greece, and his wife CLYTEMNESTRA. When the Greek fleet was ready to set sail for Troy in order to rescue HELEN, they were delayed at Aulis by contrary winds. The goddess ARTEMIS was angry with Agamemnon for killing her favorite stag and only the sacrifice of Iphigenia would appease her and cause the wind to change. At first Agamemnon refused and ordered all the Greeks to return to their homes, but he was finally persuaded to consent. Iphigenia was summoned to Aulis on the pretext of marriage to ACHILLES and all was prepared for the sacrifice. At the last moment Artemis took pity on the girl and substituted a stag, bearing Iphigenia off to be her priestess at Taurica, where she was charged with sacrificing all strangers to the goddess. This she did until she recognized her brother ORESTES as one of the potential victims; she revealed herself to him and they fled together.

ISHKUR see ADAD

ISHTAR

(Sumerian Inanna), the most important of all Mesopotamian goddesses, and a multi-faceted personality, occurring in cuneiform texts of all periods. The Sumerian name probably means 'Lady of Heaven', and the Akkadian name Ishtar is related to the Syrian Astarte and the biblical Ashtaroth. Ishtar is usually considered as a daughter of ANZU, with her cult located in Uruk, but there are other traditions as to her ancestry, and it is probable that these reflect originally different goddesses that were identified with her. Ishtar is the subject of a cycle of texts describing her love affair and ultimately fatal relationship with TAMMUZ. She is also generally the goddess of love and sex,

Right Ishtar as the 'Lady of Heaven' holding the sun and the crescent moon and seated on a lion, from a Sassanian silver dish.

and textual evidence exists to indicate her general connection with cult prostitution. She is also important as a goddess of war, who accompanies kings in battle, ablaze with excitement. Ishtar is also known to be the planet Venus. Her early symbol is a reed bundle.

ISIS

Egyptian goddess whose two major characteristics were her magical powers and her link with the throne of Egypt as the symbolic mother of the pharaoh. Isis can be shown wearing the symbol of the throne or the headdress of cow-horns and sun disk. Her genealogy was the same as that of OSIRIS – to whom she was both sister and wife – in that she was the child of GEB and NUT. In a Golden Age she ruled over Egypt by Osiris' side. When Osiris was murdered by SETH she sought out his body and with her wings revived him sufficiently to become pregnant with HORUS, whom she brought up safely in the Delta marshes, guarding him from the threat of Seth. She protected him against scorpions, snakes and fevers, and was consequently involved whenever a child suffered from poisonous bites or fever. Magical spells survive to show that a sick child was identified with Horus so that the magic of Isis could cure the ailment.

The magic of Isis was powerful enough to cajole the sun god RE into revealing his secret name; this knowledge gave the person aware of it power over the bearer of that name. She caught some of the saliva dribbled to earth by the sun god and mixed it with clay to form a serpent, which in turn stung the god, who became seriously ill with his own poison. Isis, summoned to effect a cure, refused unless Re revealed his secret name. The sun god prevaricated and reeled off a list of names and epithets but Isis realized that his secret name was not included. The poison burned more intensely and at last Re, binding Isis by oath not to divulge his secret name any further than to her son Horus, revealed the powerful knowledge to the goddess.

In the Hellenistic and Roman period the cult of Isis took on a new form as a mystery religion. Some of its rituals were revealed in paintings at Pompeii and Herculaneum, and also in *The Golden Ass* of Apuleius, a Roman north African writer of the second century AD. Her temples spread across the Mediterranean to the Acropolis at Athens and to the island of Delos. In Egypt itself the temple of Isis on the island of Philae, just south of the First Cataract of the Nile at Aswan, was the last to hold out against the advent of Christianity, not being surpressed until the reign of the sixth-century Byzantine Emperor Justinian.

Left The Egyptian goddess Isis in her Romanized form as a cool classical draped figure.

Below The Romans adapted and expanded the cult of Isis; this wall painting from Herculaneum shows the priests of Isis performing their afternoon service, the ceremony of the water.

JANUS

A legendary king who was reputed to be the first ruler of Italy. He founded a small town on the River Tiber which he called the Janiculum, still the name of one of the seven hills of Rome. During his reign SATURN fled to Italy, driven from heaven by his son JUPITER, and Janus welcomed him and made him co-ruler. He is represented with two faces looking in opposite directions, because he knew both past and future. His double-gated temple in the forum in Rome had an additional symbolic significance; the gates remained closed in peace and were only opened in time of war. Janus later developed into a god of all beginnings; the month of January was sacred to him, while as four-headed Janus, or Janus Quadrifons, he presided over the four seasons.

JASON

Son of Aeson and leader of the ARGONAUTS. When Aeson's father, Cretheus died, Aeson's half-brother Pelias, son of Poseidon and Cretheus' wife Tyro, usurped the throne, allowing Aeson to live in Iolcus as a private citizen. Not trusting Pelias, Jason's parents smuggled him out of Iolcos under cover of a mock funeral and a report of his death, and gave him to the centaur CHIRON to be reared in his care. Meanwhile Pelias was warned

by the Delphic oracle to beware of a descendant of Aeolus (the great-grandfather of Jason) who would appear wearing only one sandal.

When he reached manhood Jason left Mount Pelion where the centaur lived and returned to Iolcos strangly dressed in a tiger skin and with a lance in each hand. Thus attired he arrived in the main square of Iolcos just as Pelias was offering a sacrifice. Significantly Jason wore one sandal only, the other having been lost when he helped an old lady (Hera, who hated Pelias for his neglect of her rites) to cross the River Anauros.

Pelias was alarmed at Jason's return and when, on the sixth day, Jason called on Pelias and claimed the power that was his by right, Pelias ordered him to bring the fleece of the ram which had magically carried Phrixus, son of Creutheus' brother Athamas to Colchis. Pelias was certain that Jason would not return since the Golden Fleece was guarded by a dragon. In return for the fleece, Pelias agreed to name Jason his successor. This was a clever move since he was caught in a dilemma: on the one hand he could not harm the young man in festival time, especially since he probably enjoyed the support of many people, and on the other he represented a serious threat not only to Pelias' throne but even to his life.

Jason consulted the Delphic oracle and gathered around him a band of the noblest heroes in Greece, the ARGONAUTS, some of whom had been boyhood friends on Mount Pelion. Besides HERACLES there were specialists such as Argos the shipbuilder, Tiphys the pilot, Lynceus who had marvelous eyesight, ORPHEUS with the magical powers of his music and Polydeuces the boxer. The witch MEDEA, Aeetes'

Far left Bronze statuette of Jove the Thunderer, father of the Roman gods, throned in majesty and holding a scepter and thunderbolt.

Above The *Argo* , in which Jason and the Argonauts undertook the quest for the Golden Fleece, may have looked something like this Roman representation of a ship.

Right This unusual Roman bronze shows the mask of Juno Lucina, Juno in her aspect as goddess of childbirth. Its non-classical mood may be explained by the fact that it was found in Hungary, a far-flung outpost of the Roman Empire.

daughter, gave Jason indispensable help in winning the Golden Fleece and when he returned from Colchis, he married her and gave the fleece to Pelias. At this point the traditions diverge dramatically, some saying that Jason ruled instead of Pelias, some that he lived quietly in Iolcos. One story is that Medea by her magic caused the death of Pelias, persuading his daughters to boil him in a cauldron on the grounds that this would rejuvenate him – which of course it did not.

After Pelias' death, Jason and Medea were driven from Iolcos by Pelias' son. After ten years together in Corinth, Jason transferred his affection from Medea to Glauce, daughter of King Creon. Medea murdered the two children she had had by Jason and fled into the sky in a chariot. Jason met his death when part of the stern of the Argo fell on him whilst he was sleeping.

JUNO

A Roman goddess of marriage and the long-suffering wife of JUPITER. Like her Greek equivalent, HERA, she was the protector of women, in particular married women. A festival took place in her honor on the calends (first) of March. When referred to as Juno Lucina she was the goddess of childbirth. Those making offerings to her had to untie any knots about their person, since these could hinder a safe delivery. As Juno Moneta she governed finance, and the Roman mint was located in her temple on the Capitoline Hill. Juno's name is the feminine counterpart of Jupiter (Heavenly Father) and, whereas all men had their 'Genius', all women had their 'Juno'.

JUPITER

The Roman equivalent of ZEUS, he came to hold the predominant position in the Roman pantheon, appearing as the god of the sky, of daylight, of the weather and, particularly, of thunder and lightning. He came to hold this position partly through his identification with Zeus and partly through the assistance he offered ROMULUS in driving back the Sabines. Romulus established a temple to Jupiter at the spot where he had first implored his assistance. With his temple on the Capitol, Jupiter was seen as the supreme power whose priest (*flamen Dialis*) was married to the priestess of Juno (*flaminica*). It was to Jupiter that newly-elected consuls offered their first prayers, and it was he who oversaw international relations through the mediation of the college of priests. The establishment of a Capitol, similar to that at Rome, in every provincial city affirmed the political bond between Rome as mother city and the daughters which were all a copy of her.

Left Jupiter Ammon; the majesty of the father of the Roman gods, with flowing beard and solemn aspect, is here combined with ram's horns and ears. Ammon was the site of one of the most celebrated oracles of Jupiter.

Below Temple to Jupiter, Juno and Minerva, the Capitoline Triad, in the Roman Capitol at Dougga, Tunisia. Wherever the conquering Roman armies went, their principal deities were established.

KHEPRI

In Egyptian mythology the scarab beetle was a form of the sun god synonymous with the idea of ancient Egypt itself, representing the sun at dawn emerging above the mountains of the eastern horizon. The ancient Egyptians observed that scarab beetles pushed around huge balls of dirt and so made the analogy that the sun in the sky could be propeled across the firmament by a gigantic scarab beetle. They also observed that from the ball of dirt a young scarab emerged spontaneously, a fitting image for a creator god who arose out of the primeval water self-generated, hence the name Khepri or 'He who is coming into being'. Jewelry from ancient Egypt often included a scarab carved out of semi-precious stones.

KHNUM

In Egyptian mythology the ram god Khnum was a creator god who molded the human race on a potter's wheel. In a hymn from his cult temple at Esna which reads like an anatomy lesson, every part of a human being owes its existence to Khnum's expertise. Khnum was in addition an important god presiding over the Cataract regions of the river Nile. It was at his behest that HAPY, god of the Inundation, rose from his caverns at Aswan.

KHONSU

In Egyptian mythology the moon god, child of the union of AMUN-RE and MUT at Thebes. His name means 'wanderer' and refers to the most erratic cycle of the moon in the sky when compared to the course of the sun god. Khonsu could be hawk-headed or take the form of a child wearing the sidelock of youth and wore a crown showing the disk of the full moon resting between the horns of the crescent moon. Khonsu played an integral part in the New Year celebrations at Thebes when his statue accompanied those of his parents to the temple of Luxor, leaving its normal abode in his temple just to the south of Amun's at Karnak. He also had a manifestation as a god of healing and exorcism. In the reign of Rameses II (1290-1224 BC) his statue was transported from Thebes to Bakhtar to drive out a malevolent spirit from the princess Bentresh, and was only returned to Thebes after four years.

Far left   The ram god Khnum followed by the goddess Sakhmet.

Above   The giant scarab beetle creator god Khepri.

Below   Temple at Luxor, Egypt, sacred to Amun, Mut and Khonsu.

113

LACHESIS

LEDA

One of the Greek Fates (Moirai) represented from the time of Homer as three old women spinning out men's destinies like thread. The three were called Clotho ('the spinner'), who held the distaff, Lachesis ('the apportioner') who drew off the thread, and Atropos ('the inflexible') who cut it short. A person's apportionment may govern what happens to him in life, but most often refers to his death, since death is everyone's portion. In mythology the Fates played little part. Their relationship with the gods is variable. Thus they aided ZEUS in his battles both against the giants and against Typhon. They persuaded the latter, when he was already under pressure from Zeus, to eat a diet of human food, assuring him, contrary to the truth, that it would strengthen him. APOLLO, on the other hand, cheated the Fates, making them drunk, so allowing his friend Admetus to live beyond his alloted span providing that he could find a substitute to meet death in his place.

According to the most familiar tradition, Leda was a daughter of Thestius, king of Aetolia, and married Tyndareus, king of Sparta. However, some of her children were fathered by ZEUS. These are normally given as HELEN of Troy and either both the DIOSCURI (Castor and Pollux) or else just Pollux alone. The parentage of Helen is subject to debate; it was said that she was really the daughter of Zeus and the goddess NEMESIS. In order to avoid Zeus' advances, Nemesis is said to have changed herself into many different forms, including a goose. Zeus transformed himself into a swan and their embrace provided a favorite classical and Renaissance artistic subject. Nemesis abandoned the egg which resulted from their union and it was picked up by a herdsman who took it to Leda (in most accounts). When Helen hatched from it, Leda claimed her for her own on account of Helen's great beauty. However, from the time of Euripedes onward it was accepted that Leda gave birth to one egg (or occasionally two)

Far left The three Fates, Atropos, Clotho and Lachesis, spinning out each man's allotted portion of life, are used in this sixteenth century Flemish tapestry to illustrate Petrarch's *Triumph of Death over Chastity*.

Left Zeus disguised as a swan seduces the not wholly reluctant Leda on this Roman tombstone from Crete. Many of Zeus's amours were conducted in unexpected forms.

Above The Avenue of Lions on the island of Delos, Greece, where Leto finally gave birth to her twins Apollo and Artemis, the children of Zeus. The jealous Hera pursued Leto for nine days and nine nights before finally allowing her to come to rest on Delos. Throughout the classical period the island was uninhabited except for priests; celebrants took ship from the neighboring island of Rinia and were housed in hostels, the remains of which are still visible.

as a result of her own love for Zeus. The two pairs of children were Pollux and CLYTEMNESTRA, Helen and Castor.

The story of the egg is, in all probability, related to a Minoan-Mycenaean tale of deities in bird shape. Although later writers either disbelieved or ridiculed the story, fragments of the enormous shell were preserved at the temple of Leucippidae in Sparta.

LETO

One of the Titans (the first generation of Greek gods), she was the daughter of the Titan Coeus and Phoebe and mother to the twin gods, APOLLO and ARTEMIS, whose father was ZEUS. Knowing that Leto's children would be greater than her own, the jealous HERA constrained Leto to travel far and wide in search of a sheltered place where she might bear her divine twins. Finally the barren island of Ortygia received her and, because the god of light first saw daylight there, changed its name to Delos, the Brilliant. A different legend claimed the birth to have taken place on the island of Poseidon, where Zeus created a screen against the sun's rays by forming

a wave-shaped arch out of seawater. Leto's birth pains lasted nine days and nine nights on account of the fact that Hera delayed the arrival of Eileithyia (the goddess of childbirth) for some time. Apollo and Artemis later took vengeance on Hera and other persecutors of their mother.

LOKI

God of fire and mischief maker among the Norse gods. It was not pleasant mischief either; he was invariably malicious but, having caused harm, he would then often by his wiles put matters right either of his own accord or under duress from the other gods. He was the proverbial sore-thumb among the gods of Asgard and only seems to be tolerated because of an obscure blood-brotherhood relationship with ODIN. He had two brothers, but they are of little account.

It was through his children that Loki caused most trouble and Odin knew that they would be triumphant at the Ragnarok, the Doom of the Gods. Loki's wife was the goddess Sigyn and by her he had two sons, Nari and Vali. He also had a relationship with an ogress called Angrboda and she produced three children. First was FENRIR the Wolf, second was Jormungandr, the World Serpent, and third was a daughter, Hel, who became Queen of the Underworld.

Loki's mischief, stealing and evil exasperated the gods. He helped the Giants to kidnap the goddess Idun, enticing her out of Asgard to a wood where she could be captured, together with the magic apples that ensured the gods stayed ever young. The gods immediately began to age and, realizing that Loki was at the bottom of this mischief, they threatened him until he told the truth and he was made to get the goddess and her apples back. Another time he stole FREYA's magic necklace Brisingamen. Another mischief was when he cut off all the goddess Sif's golden hair. She was the wife of THOR, who threatened to break every bone in Loki's body until Loki promised that he would make good by going to work with the Dark Elves and make hair of spun gold that would become real when it was put to Sif's head.

His greatest misdeed was to bring about the death of BALDER by duping the blind god HODER. It was after Balder's death that the gods decided to bind Loki once and for all. As with his evil offspring the wolf Fenrir, they had problems in finding suitable material to restrain him. Finally they succeeded by using the entrails of Loki's son Nari, who had just been eviscerated by his brother Vali in wolf guise. As Loki lay bound underground, poison was dripped on to his face from serpents fastened above him. His faithful wife Sigyn caught the venom in a dish to shield him but each time the dish was full she had to turn away to empty it and the venom fell on his face. His agonized writhing caused earthquakes and volcanic eruptions.

Eventually, as Odin knew, Loki, the personification of fire and evil, would bring about the Doom of the Gods, leading the fearful giants into Asgard and destroying everything with fire sweeping through earth and heaven. Loki's status in Asgard in the Norse myths is a curious one. Tolerated because of his blood-brotherhood relationship with Odin he is, nevertheless, the canker in their midst that leads to their fall.

LOUCETIUS

Unusual among the Celtic warrior dieties as he sometimes appears with a consort, NEMETONA. His name means 'the shining one' and hers 'the goddess of the sacred grove'. Although known from dedications across Europe, he appears to come from the area of Trier, Germany, and a dedication to him and his consort, *Loucetio Marti et Nemetona*, from Bath (Aquae Sulis), England, was made by a native of Trier. Loucetius is also associated with MARS, as in the Bath inscription, on a relief from Altripp, Pfalz, Germany, emphasizing in this instance the healing as well as the martial aspects of the god.

LUCRETIA

While engaged on a siege at Ardrea, Lucretia's husband, Tarquinius Collatinus, and his fellow commanders rode back to Rome to test the loyalty of their wives. One of the commanders, Sextus Tarquinius, was so aroused by Lucretia's beauty and virtue that he later burst into her room and raped her. Summoning her husband, father and other nobles to avenge this crime, she stabbed herself. According to Roman legend, this incident resulted in the insurrection led by Junius Brutus and the expulsion of the Tarquins from Rome. The story is told by Livy and is the subject of Shakespeare's poem *The Rape of Lucrece* (1594).

Left The west face of the monumental tenth century AD stone cross at Gosforth, northern England, shows details of the last battle of the Norse gods, Ragnarok. At the foot is Loki bound beneath the poisonous serpent, his wife Sigyn emptying the poison from a cup. Above them is Odin on horseback, while at the top Heimdall, guardian of the heavens, is attacked by two dragons. Ragnarok ends in the destruction of the Norse world and the founding of a new and purer universe.

MAET

Egyptian goddess whose name is frequently translated as 'Truth' but who was more universal in that she personified the balanced order established by the sun god, whose daughter she was, at the time of creation. She was the antithesis of the chaotic forces of 'non-existence' that threatened to crash through the sky and destroy the world. Maet's symbol was the ostrich feather. In her name the hieroglyph of a sloping plinth represented the primeval mound. The throne of OSIRIS often rested upon the plinth of Maet, and in the world of the living in Egypt the pharaoh derived his authority to govern by upholding the laws of Maet. A crucial scene in Egyptian temple decoration shows the monarch presenting the effigy of Maet, as a seated woman wearing a feather on her head, to the major deity of the sanctuary. In the Hall of the Two Truths in the Underworld the goddess was the counter-weight to the claims of the heart of the dead person in the scales before the 42 assessor gods. See also AMMUT.

MAPONUS

'The divine youth' is, to judge from the six dedications known to him, an important Romano-Celtic military god. All were made by senior officers in the Roman army in North Britain. One of them, a small crescentic silver votive inscribed *Deo Mapono*, was found at the fort of Vindolanda and possibly indicates the location of a shrine to the god. The attributes associated with him are hunting, healing, poetry and music. An altar from Hexham equates him with Apollo Cithareodus – Apollo the Lyre Player, an aspect of the god well known from statues in the classical world. All the attributes given to Maponus are also those of APOLLO and on several of the dedications he is associated with Apollo. No fully identifiable representations of Maponus are known because on the several altars where he is represented with Apollo, the side on which he occurs has, through fate over the centuries, been defaced or destroyed. Nevertheless, he remains a potent god and one who must originally have been an important Celtic solar deity.

Far left The palace of King Minos of Crete at Knossos.

Above Head of Maponus carved in the Celtic idiom.

Below left and right Maet, Egyptian goddess of balance and harmony.

Right This Babylonian monster with its horned lion's head and scaly body is one manifestation of Marduk who, in the Babylonian creation epic, saved the gods from destruction and was annually reinstated as their king in some form of rebirth cycle.

MARDUK

A major Mesopotamian god, his name being derived from the Sumerian Amar-utu, 'Bullcalf-of-Utu', and city god of the town of Babylon, which from the reign of Hammurabi (1792-1750 BC) became the capital of southern Mesopotamia, with a corresponding upgrading of Marduk's previously obscure status. This received a permanent boost when Nebuchadnezzar I (1124-1103 BC) fought a successful campaign against the Elamites and recaptured the statue of Marduk that had been plundered by them under Kudur-Nahhunte, an event that is treated in several important inscriptions, and a turning point in the religious history of Mesopotamia. The religious reform that took place under Nebuchadnezzar I saw the supremacy of Marduk, which lasted down to the end of the cuneiform epoch. Marduk lived in the temple Esagil in Babylon with his spouse Zarpanitu. At the period of the Neo-Babylonian kings such as Nebuchadnezzar II (604-562 BC) he was regarded as the head of the pantheon, and Nabu, the god of writing and city god of nearby Borsippa, was regarded as his son.

Marduk was especially associated with magic and is named in many spells and incantations, sometimes under the name Asalluhi, originally the god of the city Ku'ara, with whom he became identified. In *Enuma Elish*, the Babylonian creation epic, it was Marduk who conquered Tiamat and saved the gods from destruction, although in Assyrian sources this was attributed to the Assyrian national god, Assur. The gods EA and Anu had failed against Tiamat, so the young Marduk undertook the battle in exchange for recognition as the representative of the gods, with civic and military powers and the power of life and death. His successful conquest of Tiamat led to his creation of the cosmos from her body. The gods proclaimed him as king and their leader, and one tablet of the epic is devoted to a learned and laudatory exposition of the fifty names of Marduk. Marduk was annually reinstated as king of the gods in the New Year rites held in the Akitu House when the creation epic was recited.

In the first millennium BC Marduk was often referred to as Bel, 'Lord'. The increasing synchronization of Marduk with the other important gods of the pantheon is exemplified in a small cuneiform tablet that explains each god as a particular aspect of Marduk himself, eg. NINURTA is Marduk of the pick, and this has been seen by some scholars as a move towards monotheism. His particular symbols are the pointed triangular spade, found commonly on cylinder seals and boundary stones, and the mythical beast called mushhushshu. This is a composite leonine monster with a horned snake's head, scaly body and eagle's talons (probably taken over from the god Tishpak of Eshnunna when Hammurabi defeated that city), well-known from the glazed brick representations found on the Ishtar Gate at Babylon, built by Nebuchadnezzar II.

MARS

Roman god of war and agriculture and the most important god after JUPITER, Mars was equated with the Greek god ARES and was consequently regarded as the son of JUNO. The Romans believed that the goddess Juno bore Mars after she had been impregnated by a flower, whereas the Greeks attributed the paternity of Ares to ZEUS. Mars' fatherhood of ROMULUS by RHEA SILVIA, a Vestal Virgin, founded the Roman race. He had come to Rhea Silvia while she was asleep and she bore him Romulus and REMUS.

Mars' functions appear to have evolved as the Romans themselves evolved from an agricultural to a warlike nation. Since the month named after the god, March (originally the first month of the Roman year), saw both the rebirth of the agricultural year and the start of the campaigning season, the combination of his functions was natural to an agricultural people increasingly engaged in war. Mars had his own priest and altar at Rome and his sacred animals were the wolf and the wood-

pecker. A number of festivals were dedicated to him, among them a horse race (14 March) and the purification of the sacred trumpets (23 March) originally used in war. His festival in October indicates a time when both soldiers and farmers would lay aside their tools and weapons. Mars' love for VENUS was early established as a favorite subject for artists.

Left This splendid first century AD statue of Mars, Roman god of war, in full imperial battle regalia, fully justifies the epithet 'martial'.

Below Mars in a more pacific aspect, though still wielding spear and shield and wearing his war helm, from the House of the Marine Venus at Pompeii. The exquisite wall paintings of Pompeii are remarkable for their celebration of animal, plant and marine life.

Right This sixteenth century Italian plate shows the sorceress Medea borne away in her dragon-drawn chariot, while her minions prepare the magic cauldron for the miserable Pelias – although it seems doubtful whether he will survive to be placed in it.

MARSYAS

A Phrygian satyr. Having invented the flute, ATHENA put a curse on it and threw it away in disgust when she saw, in a reflection of herself in water, how distorted her cheeks were when playing it. Marsyas, on finding the flute, was so captivated by the beauty of its sound that he challenged APOLLO to make music of equal beauty on his lyre. The first trial resulting in a draw, Apollo challenged Marsyas to play his flute upside down. The Muses adjudged Apollo the victor and Marsyas was tied to a tree and flayed alive, the blood or else the tears of his friends the satyrs forming the river Marsyas. Afterwards Apollo so regreted his anger that he broke his lyre. The flaying of Marsyas was a theme frequently used by classical vase painters and western artists.

MEDEA

'The cunning one' in mythology, daughter of Aeetes king of the Colchians and his wife the Oceanid Eidyia, granddaughter of Helios and niece of CIRCE. She is universally said to have been a witch but is also sometimes seen as a goddess. A much later legend, related by Diodorus, informs us that Medea was a princess of great humanity.

When JASON arrived at Colchis with the ARGO-NAUTS in his quest for the Golden Fleece, HERA, who wished to punish Pelias, king of Iolcos, made Medea fall passionately in love with Jason, then she used her magical powers to assist Jason in his quest for the Golden Fleece. She gave him a magic ointment making him impervious to the attacks of the fire-breathing bulls, told him how to defeat the soldiers who would spring from the dragon's teeth and drugged, or killed, the serpent which guarded the Golden Fleece. She also engineered the Argonauts' escape from Aeetes. In one version of the story she murdered and cut into pieces her younger brother Apsyrtus, scattering the fragments so that her father might be delayed in his pursuit of the Argonauts when he stopped to pick up the pieces of body. In other versions Apsyrtus is grown up and leads the pursuit until Medea tricks him into an interview with Jason, who treacherously murders him. Circe later purified the pair of their guilt but on hearing the details of their crime afflicted them with a curse. Later in their journey Medea helped Jason by killing Talos, the bronze man of Crete, who protected the island for MINOS by running around it thrice a day preventing intruders from landing. Medea removed the nail – lodged in his heel – which stopped up his great vein, and he bled to death.

At Iolcos Medea took vengeance on Pelias (Jason's uncle) for the wrong done by him to Jason's family. First she restored Aeson, Jason's father, to youth by boiling him in a cauldron of magic herbs and then persuaded the daughters of Pelias to submit their father to a similar treatment, only this time Media provided inefficacious herbs. In retaliation for the death of Pelias by this trick, Acastrus, his son, drove Jason and Medea from Iolcos and they took refuge in Corinth. At this point the stories diverge markedly, the most famous being found in the tragedy of Euripedes first produced in 431 BC. In Euripedes we find Jason tired of Medea and arranging to marry the daughter of Creon, king of Corinth. Medea's anger is aroused and, fearing her vengeance upon him and his daughter, Creon banishes Medea and her two children. Coaxing him into allowing her a respite of one day, Medea kills Jason's bride and Creon and goes on to kill Jason's children. Finally, taunting Jason in his despair, she escapes to Athens. The story was used by Cherubini in his opera *Medea* of 1797.

Left Medea as the gracious princess with whom Jason fell in love, from a wall painting at Herculaneum. Appearances are deceptive, however; Medea is one of the most cruel and bloodthirsty characters in the admittedly blood-spattered canons of classical mythology.

MEDUSA

One of the three GORGONS, the only one who was mortal. Anyone who looked at her head, even after her death, was turned to stone. Medusa was hated by ATHENA for making love to POSEIDON in a temple dedicated to her. Athena therefore appeared to PERSEUS and presented him with a bronze shield and instructions on how to bring about the death of Medusa. Using a cap of invisibility, Perseus flew over the ocean and found the Gorgons. Keeping clear of the other Gorgons, Stheno and Euryale who were immortal, he advanced towards Medusa, watching her reflection in his bronze shield. Striking off Medusa's head with Hermes' sword, and hiding it in his wallet, Perseus successfully fled from her sisters.

MELEAGER

At his birth, the Fates declared that Meleager should continue to live as long as a log that was on the fire was not consumed. His mother, Althaia, preserved this brand. Some time later Meleager's father, Oeneus, king of Calydon, omitted to sacri-

Above This winged Medusa figure with her mad glare and writhing snakes decorates an antefix, part of the roofing system, on an Etruscan temple, to prevent malign influences entering the sanctuary.

Right Medusa the Gorgon as a terrifying grinning figure about to meet her fate at the hands of Perseus, who looks firmly away so as not to be turned to stone. Athena stands supportively behind him, while from Medusa's blood the winged horse Pegasus is born. This architectural sculpture comes from the ancient temple at Selinunte, Sicily, and is carved in the static but effective archaic style.

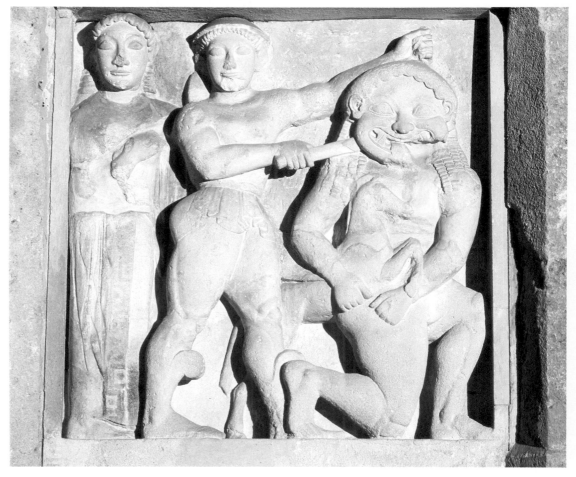

fice to ARTEMIS who, in her anger, sent a huge boar to ravage Calydon. Meleager killed the boar and gave the skin as a trophy to the virgin huntress ATALANTA, who had been the first to wound it. Meleager's maternal uncles then tried to steal the trophy from Atalanta, whereupon they were killed by Meleager. Hearing of this Althaia burned the brand which she had preserved, thereby causing the death of Meleager. The hunt of the Calydonian boar was a favorite subject in Hellenistic art.

MENELAUS

In Greek myth king of Sparta, son of ATREUS, younger brother of AGAMEMNON and husband of HELEN, whom PARIS carried off to Troy, thus bringing about the expedition of the Greek chiefs to recover her in the Trojan War. Menelaus and Helen lived peacefully in Sparta until Helen was abducted by Paris while Menelaus was attending the funeral of his grandfather Catreus in Crete. Receiving the news, Menelaus returned to Sparta and gathered around him all those who had unsuccessfully sought Helen's hand in marriage.

When Helen and her father, Tyndareus, had chosen Menelaus, Tyndareus made them all swear an oath to help the successful suitor if ever he needed it. Menelaus took part in an expedition of sixty ships under the command of Agamemnon, and, with the blessing of HERA, who had aligned herself with Menelaus and united all the Greeks against Paris, her personal enemy.

In the *Iliad*, Menelaus features prominently in the dramatic events at Troy – while the Trojans mocked him for his cowardice, he is portrayed as courageous by Homer. Menelaus agreed to settle the dispute by means by a duel with Paris. He defeated Paris but was prevented from killing him when APHRODITE carried him off on a cloud. Agamemnon pointed out to the Trojans who were watching the fight that his brother was clearly the victor and demanded that Helen be restored to him. As the Trojans hesitated, Pandarus fired an arrow at Menelaus and grazed him in an attempt to prevent the Trojan War from ending. A general battle then broke out in which Menelaus showed considerable bravery, in particular in rescuing the corpse of PATROCLUS.

Menelaus appeared again in the events subsequent to the *Iliad*. Upon Paris' death he had his corpse mutilated. Later Menelaus appears among the warriors inside the Wooden Horse. There are several conflicting accounts of the eventual meeting of Menelaus with Helen, and of ODYSSEUS' role in this meeting. Menelaus might or might not have sought revenge on Helen for betraying him by marrying the Trojan Deiphobus after the death of Paris. Perhaps the most dramatic account shows Helen seeking refuge at the household altar. Intending to slay her, Menelaus burst in on her with raised sword only to be so captivated by his wife's beauty that he fell deeply in love with her again. After much travelling at the mercy of the elements, Menelaus and Helen arrived in Sparta, eight years after leaving Troy, and some eighteen after the start of the war. At the end of his life, Menelaus was carried off to the Elysian fields.

MERCURY

A Roman god, son of Maia and JUPITER and introduced at an early date from a Greek or Graeco-Etruscan source. He is closely identified with the Greek god HERMES, the messenger of Jupiter whose attributes – the *caduceus* (wand), broad-rimmed hat, winged sandals and purse – he shares. Like Hermes, he protected merchants; indeed his name contains the root of the word *merx*, meaning merchandise.

Above The late thirteenth century BC Warrior Vase from Mycenae, Greece, shows what the Greek army led by Menelaus and Agamemnon, which waged war on the Trojans for ten long years, probably looked like.

Right Mercury, Roman messenger god, wearing his characteristic broad-rimmed hat and bearing his staff or *caduceus*.

MERET-SEGER

In Egyptian mythology the cobra goddess dwelling on the peak overlooking the tombs of the pharaohs in the Valley of the Kings; the name Meretseger means 'She who loves silence'. The official tombworkers who lived in the village of Deir el Medina regarded Meretseger as a dangerous goddess who could violently react against anyone guilty of perjury or related crimes by causing him to go blind or fall ill through a venemous bite.

Left Mercury in a more down-to-earth setting, providing the water source for a fountain in the streets of the Roman town of Pompeii.

Above Minerva, Roman goddess of wisdom, in the center of a silver medallion cup from the Hildesheim treasure, surrounded by a palm and acanthus garland. Note the quality of the carving and the unusually high relief – the goddess's foot and helmet extend to three-dimensional effect into the decorative surround.

MIDAS

Midas, the legendary king of Phrygia, having entertained Silenus, the companion of DIONYSUS, who had lost his way, was granted a wish. He wished that all he touched might turn to gold, but upon discovering that this applied also to his food, Midas asked to be relieved of his wish. He was instructed to wash in the river Paetolus which, ever since has had sands containing gold. A different strand of the myth would have it that Midas was so curious to learn the wisdom of Silenus that he made him drunk by mixing wine with his water. He was then told a parable to the effect that riches do not bring happiness. A related myth is that told by Plutarch. Lost in the desert, Midas is granted relief for his thirst by a spring of gold, which was turned by Dionysus into a fountain called, accordingly, the spring of Midas.

MIN

Egyptian fertility god and the symbol of procreative sexuality. He was shown wearing a tall plumed crown, balancing a flagellum on his fingertips, his phallus proudly announcing his readiness for sexual union. He was the guardian god of nomads and hunters and his particular domain was the eastern desert. The festival of Min, commemorated on Theban mortuary temples, was a ceremony of celebrating fecundity in nature and the regeneration of life in a way that hinted at the royal jubilee of rejuvenation rituals.

MINERVA

The Roman goddess of crafts and trade – and of the intellectual activity necessary to their successful practice – Minerva was identified with the Greek goddess Pallas ATHENA and took over her martial characteristics. Together with Jupiter and Juno she was one of the great Capitoline triad and was introduced to Rome by an Etruscan contingent which came to the aid of ROMULUS. Minerva's festival was the Quinquartrus (19 March). She plays no part in any specifically Roman legend.

MINOS

Legendary king of Crete, said to have lived three generations before the Trojan War. He was the son of EUROPA and ZEUS and was brought up by Asterion, king of Crete, after whose death he became the sole ruler of Crete, raising up a bull from the sea to prove his right to the succession. Minos' reign was one of justice and equity. Indeed his laws were considered so remarkable that they were thought to have been directly inspired by Zeus, whom he is said to have consulted every nine years. This portrayal of Minos in Greek myth is in contrast to the Attic legends which cast him as an evil figure exacting tribute from Athens, as told in the story of THESEUS, who was aided in his defeat of the MINOTAUR and escape from Crete by Minos' daughter ARIADNE. The discrepancy is probably explained by a real contest between Attica and Crete. Having expeled his brother, Rhadamanthys, Minos initiated his legislative ideas. In the Underworld both Minos and Rhadamanthys sat in judgment over the souls of the dead, assisted by Aeacus. Minos was a womanizer, but was also supposed to be the originator of homosexuality. He was killed in his bath by one of the daughters of DAEDALUS, king of Sicily.

MINOTAUR

A monster with a bull's head and a man's body, the son of PASIPHAE, wife of King Minos of Crete, and the bull sent to Minos by POSEIDON. Minos had the Athenian architect, DAEDALUS, construct a vast palace (the Labyrinth) comprising such a maze of rooms that only the architect could find his way. Shutting the monster in the labyrinth, Minos fed him seven young men and seven young women, which was the annual tribute exacted by Minos from Athens. Theseus volunteered himself to be one of the victims and, with the help of Ariadne, not only killed the Minotaur, but also found his way out of the labyrinth.

Right Throne room in the Minoan palace of Knossos, attributed to King Minos. The restored wall painting, with its floral and mythical decoration, is typical of the very advanced Minoan civilization, which lasted from the fifteenth to the twelfth centuries BC. The alabaster throne is the oldest in Europe. The palace was excavated in the nineteenth century by Sir Arthur Evans, who restored some parts to their original brilliant colors, much to the horror of some more recent archaeologists.

Below left Minoan snake goddess, probably a fertility figure.

Left Reconstruction of the bull leap fresco from the palace of Knossos. One recent theory has it that the battle of Theseus with the Minotaur was a form of bullfight.

Below right Classical Greek sculpture showing the Minotaur, the monster to which Minos's wife Pasiphae gave birth, as a noble and tragic figure, condemned to be neither man nor bull.

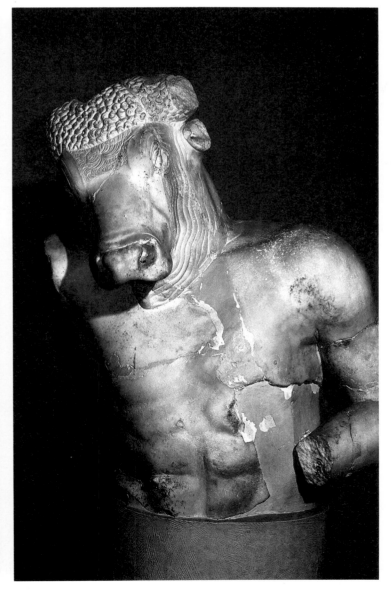

MITHRAS

An ancient Indo-Iranian god whose cult spread via Greece to the Roman world in the second half of the first century BC. The cult of Mithras, whose titles included Lord of Light, Giver of Bliss and the Victorious, proved attractive to the Roman world and in particular to its military and mercantile class. The cult was exclusively confined to men and involved initiation rites, tests and ordeals. Mithras was depicted in Roman art as a young warrior wearing the Phrygian (Persian) cap and Persian trousers. Temples to Mithras were built underground in artificial caves, recalling the cave in which Mithras was alleged to have sacrificed a bull. The cult is somewhat obscure, most of the evidence for it being from either archaeology or inscriptions.

MUT

In Egyptian mythology a mother goddess allied to the pharaoh in her aspect of the consort of AMUN, the monarch's symbolic father. She was shown as a lithe elegant woman with a vulture headdress and often wearing the double crown of Upper and Lower Egypt. Her dress was brightly colored and sometimes suggested the feathers of the vulture, a creature sacred to Mut. Mut's original nature was leonine, from which developed her association with the cat and many votive statues were dedicated to her under this form.

Above The young warrior god Mithras, in his characteristic cap and trousers, prepares to sacrifice the bull. The rough background carving represents the cave in which this event took place, and light is provided by torch-bearing initiates.

Right The Mithraeum, or temple to Mithras, below the present church of San Clemente, Rome. These temples tended to be underground, in artificial caves.

Above Two of the nine Muses from a
Roman floor mosaic of the third
century AD at El Djem, Tunisia. The
Muses were the goddesses of the
liberal arts in classical mythology. One
of their number, Calliope, was the
mother of Orpheus.

Left In this relief from the temple of
Rameses 11 at Luxor, Egypt, the mother
goddess Mut is shown in her role as
consort of Amun. She is seated behind
him wearing the double crown of
Egypt to reflect her other aspect as
protectress of the pharaoh. Khonsu,
the moon god, is the third in the
Theban triad.

NARCISSUS

A beautiful youth, son of the River Cephissus (in Boeotia) and the nymph Liriope. When he was young his mother asked the seer Tiresias whether he would live long. Tiresias answered enigmatically: 'He will if he never knows himself'. Narcissus repulsed all lovers, both men and women. Among them was ECHO who, deprived of original speech, tried to seduce Narcissus with fragments of his own speech. According to Ovid, Narcissus was punished for his cruelty to Echo when a rejected lover prayed to NEMESIS. Nemesis condemned Narcissus to the contemplation of his own beauty in a pool on Mount Helicon. The more he looked the deeper he fell in love, until finally he wasted away and died, and was turned into the narcissus flower.

NEITH

In Egyptian myth a creator goddess with a warlike aspect associated with the western Delta town of Sais. Her ancient emblem was a shield with crossed arrows and this bellicose aspect comes through in her epithet 'lady of the bow and ruler of the arrows' which made it easy for the Greeks to recognize her as their goddess ATHENA. The fullest account of Neith's role as a creator goddess can be found on the columns of Esna temple in Upper Egypt. It was at Esna according to the legend that Neith rose up out of the primeval water to create the universe. She was then carried on the Nile flood with the lates-fish (Esna was called Latopolis or 'Lates-Fishtown' in Graeco Roman times) until she reached the region of Sa el-Hagar where she founded Sais. In the Pyramid Age Neith was stated to be the mother of the crocodile god SOBEK but her role as the consort of SETH is never fully developed – at least in surviving sources.

NEKHBET

Egyptian goddess, protective deity of royalty, possessing an ancient sanctuary on the east bank of the Nile in Upper Egypt at Nekheb (modern el-Kab). She took the form of a vulture, often with her wings spread and her talons holding symbols of eternity. She symbolized the sway of kingship and, like her northern counterpart Wadjet, could appear on the crown of the pharaoh. She even adopted bovine imagery as the 'Great White Cow dwelling in Nekheb' to play the role of nurse to the royal children.

Far left Neptune and Amphitrite on a Roman mosaic from North Africa.

Below and bottom Neith in her role as a protector goddess.

Below The Egyptian goddess Nephthys, usually overshadowed by her sister Isis, here appears alone in a wooden carving from the 22nd dynasty.

Far right Here Nephthys (right) and Isis (left) are shown together kneeling before the pillar bearing the sun-disk which symbolizes the dead god Osiris, from the *Papyrus of Ani* in the Theban *Book of the Dead*.

NEMESIS

The daughter of Nyx (Night) and the personification of righteous anger, Nemesis is unusual in being both a goddess and an abstract concept. In her divine form she was pursued by ZEUS, assuming a thousand different forms in order to avoid his amorous advances (see LEDA). Finally she succumbed in the form of a goose, when he became a swan. HELEN of Troy and the DIOSCURI

were born from the resulting egg. In this legend Nemesis personifies divine vengeance. Like the Roman *Fors Fortuna*, Nemesis was charged with curbing all excess, such as excessive good fortune or the pride of kings. This reflects a fundamental concept of Greek thought that any man who rises above his condition exposes himself to divine reprisals. Thus Croesus, who was too wealthy and powerful, was enticed by Nemesis into his expedition against Cyrus, which ruined him. Nemesis was worshipped at Rhammiss in Attica, where a magnificent temple was built for her in the fifth century BC.

NEMETONA

'The goddess of the sacred grove', Nemetona is found paired with LOUCETIUS. '*Nemeton*' means sacred grove and is found incorporated into a number of place names in Gaul that presumably were connected with Nemetona or a like-named companion goddess, Arnemetia. The sacred groves were an essential element of the druidical rites and those on the island of Anglesey were specifically mentioned by Tacitus. A relief from Bath (*Aquae Sulis*), England, dedicated by Peregrinus, son of Secundus, of the Treveri (Trier, Germany), depicts the goddess with her consort Loucetius. She is seated in a long draped dress and holds a sceptre/*caduceus*-like object that leans against her left shoulder. Her right hand holds an object over a tub with encircling bands. Her consort is horned and a ram and three small hooded figures, almost *genii cucullati*, move off to the right. Water and springs seem to be, along with the sacred grove, especial associations of Nemetona.

NEPHTHYS

Egyptian goddess whose original prominence – if any – was completely overshadowed by her sister ISIS. The name of Nephthys means 'Mistress of the Mansion/Temple'. She had a minimal role as the consort of SETH but a liaison with her brother OSIRIS led to her giving birth to the jackal-god ANUBIS. Nephthys was a funerary goddess, one of the protectors of the Canopic chest containing the jars of the deceased person's viscera. Her hair tresses seem to symbolize the mummy wrappings and in the form of a kite she guarded the dead person's funerary bed in the same way as she assisted Isis to protect the couch on which Osiris lay.

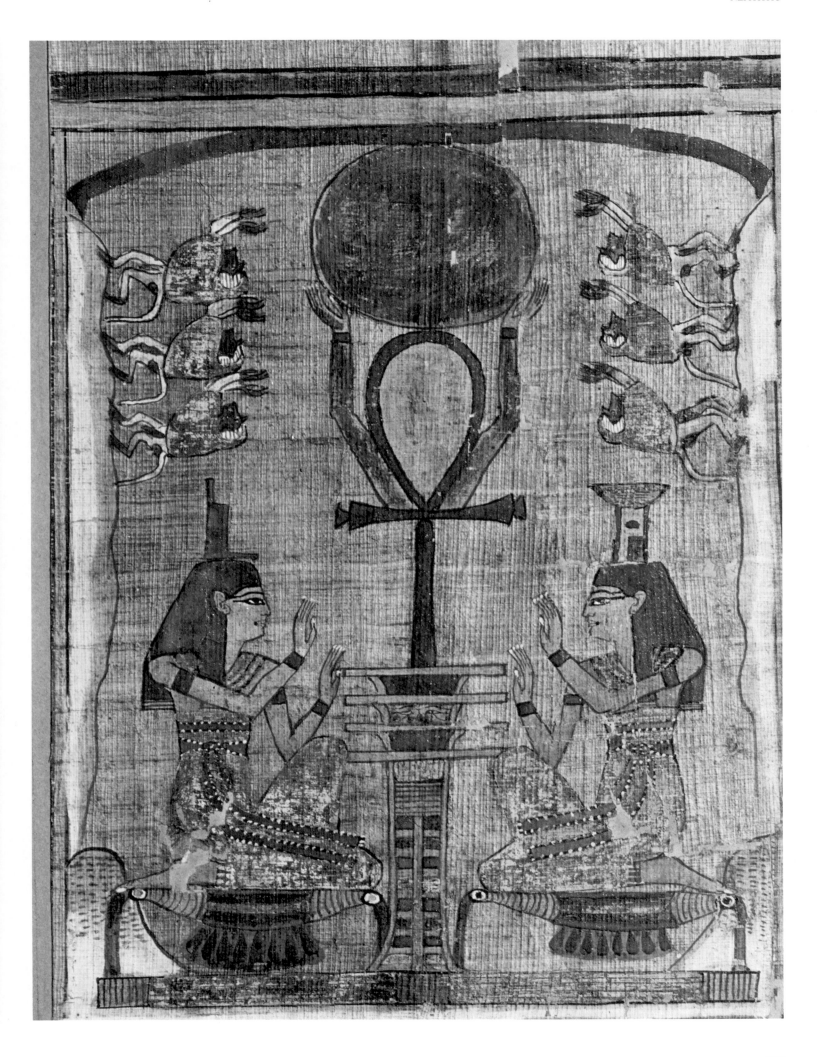

NEOPTOLE-MUS

Also known as the Young Warrior and as Pyrrhus, he was the son of ACHILLES and Deidamia, who was a daughter of Lycomedes king of Scyros. Neoptolemus was born at a time when Achilles, for his own safety, was living disguised as a girl called Pyrrha in Lycomedes' harem. Neoptolemus was brought up by his grandfather, since Achilles, his father, was engaged in the Trojan War. After his father's death ODYSSEUS was sent as a messenger to summon Neoptolemus to the siege of Troy as a necessary condition for taking the city. Concealing himself in the Trojan Horse Neoptolemus brutally killed the Trojan king PRIAM and princess Polyxena and carried off Andromache (widow of HECTOR) and Helenus, the latter's brother, as a prize.

NEPTUNE

The Roman god identified with POSEIDON. He was the god of water and, since the Romans were not in early times a seafaring people, he was a water-diety of little importance. Indeed he had no legend specific to himself until his assimilation with the Greek god Poseidon. In Roman tradition, Neptune was said to have a companion spirit called either Amphitrite, Salacia or Venilia. His festival was celebrated at the height of the summer (on 23 July) during the season of the greatest dryness.

Right This Roman mosaic from a villa near Palermo, Sicily, shows a craggy, animated Neptune, with flowing hair and beard befitting a senior god and holding the trident with which he is usually portrayed.

Left Neptune is often shown as a magisterial figure rising from the sea in a chariot drawn variously by horses and dolphins and accompanied by merfolk. On this Roman mosaic from Tunisia he also, more unusually, has a halo.

Left The head of Neptune, surrounded by a host of mythical creatures from both land and sea, decorates the center of the great silver dish which was part of the Mildenhall treasure found in Suffolk, England.

Right A Nereid or sea nymph plays with a dolphin in this charming mosaic from Roman Carthage. The Nereids were part of the kingdom of Neptune and their role was to attend the more powerful sea spirits. They had the power to disturb or calm the waters; sailors always supplicated them for a swift voyage and a prosperous return. Amphitrite, often shown as the consort of Neptune, was a Nereid.

NERGAL

An important Mesopotamian god chiefly associated with death and the Underworld, with whom several originally separate gods such as Meslamtae'a or Lugalgirra, and most especially Erra, were identified. He was the son of ENLIL and Ninlil, and in some texts he is a bellicose warrior rather similar to NINURTA. His cult city was Kutha in southern Iraq, where he was worshiped with his consort Laz in his temple Emeslam. As ruler of the realm of the dead his wife was Ereshkigal, and the *Myth of Nergal and Ereshkigal*, of which copies have been found at El Amarna in Egypt and Sultantepe in Turkey, explain the circumstances under which Nergal came to rule there. Erra was a violent deity responsible for inflicting plague on mankind, and he features prominently in the *Erra Epic*. Here Erra, briefly in control of cosmic matters in the absence of MARDUK, lays Babylonia waste with disastrous results, which have been taken to reflect historical troubles caused by the incursion of nomads into the Mesopotamian heartland.

NINHURSAG

'Lady of the Mountain', one of the Mesopotamian mother goddesses, described in Sumerian as 'mother of the gods', and 'mother of all children', and addressed as mother by many early rulers in their royal inscriptions. Other mother goddesses are mentioned in mythological and literary texts, of whom Ninmah, Nintu, Mama/Mami, and Belet-ili are perhaps the best known. Ninhursag's symbol is the uterus.

NINURTA

'Lord of the Earth', an important Sumero-Babylonian god, the son of ENLIL, worshiped especially in the city of Nippur in the temple Eshumesha. His wife is given as Gula, the goddess of healing, and since his identity is often blended with that of the god Ningirsu, sometimes also as Bau, the latter's wife. His exploits feature prominently in two lengthy bilingual (Sumerian and Akkadian) poems. The first, *King Storm whose Fearfulness is Frightful*, celebrates his defeat of the mythical monster Asag located in the mountainous areas to the east of Mesopotamia, using stones to control the water supplies for the Tigris and Euphrates rivers, and has been considered to be a nature myth primarily concerned with the age-old preoccupation with rainfall and irrigation. The second, *Fashioned Like An*, describes Ninurta's triumphant return to his city Nippur. His character is multi-sided: originally perhaps a god of the plough, venerated by farmers, it is Ninurta who imparts agricultural knowledge in a technical composition sometimes termed the *Sumerian Georgica*. His alter ego was the storm thundercloud called ANZU, who was once defeated by Ninurta according to a fragmentary myth. His prowess as a warrior is celebrated in many texts, and particularly by the later Assyrian kings; Ninurta had an important temple at Nimrud, and appears to be shown on surviving carved scenes from its walls. His symbol is the plough.

NIOBE

The name of two quite separate classical heroines. One was a daughter of the first man, Phoroneus, by the Nymph Teledice. She was ZEUS' first human mistress and bore him Argus. The other and better known was the daughter of the Lydian King Tantalus and of Dione; she married Amphione of Thebes, by whom she had seven sons and seven daughters (though the number varies from author to author). On the feast day of LETO at Thebes, she expressed scorn for Leto who had produced only two offspring, APOLLO and ARTEMIS. Affronted, Leto called on Apollo and Artemis to avenge the slight. The twin gods responded to their mother's prayers and punished Niobe's arrogance by striking down her children with their fatal arrows. She was left with one son and one daughter and, overcome with grief, she regretted her affront to Leto. In their pity the gods turned her into a rock from which flowed a spring of tears.

NODENS

The Celtic god of healing, who had an extensive cult center in a magnificent temple and associated complex at Lydney, Gloucestershire, England, above the banks of the Severn estuary. Numerous inscriptions link him with MARS, but in his healing not warlike aspect, and with NEPTUNE. Near the temple is a series of rooms or cubicles which are thought to have been used for ritual incubation, the sacred sleep, probably drug-induced, in which the god would appear to the worshipper and might heal his affliction. Dogs were also involved with the cult; their use is known from shrines in the Mediterranean world to lick wounds and abrasions to heal them. At Lydney several splendid votive representations of dogs in bronze were found, one at the bottom of a funnel in the temple center, perhaps implying a votive offered to a deity located underground.

Below This delightfully informal painting on marble from Pompeii has tragic overtones. The girls cheerfully playing knucklebones are Niobe's daughters; behind them Niobe (center) and Phoebe (on the right) try unavailingly to placate the offended Leto.

NUMA POMPILIUS

The mythical second king of Rome who, according to tradition, reigned from 715-673 BC. He was born on the same day as ROMULUS founded Rome and, on account of his piety, was invited to succeed him. He was credited with creating most of the cults and sacred institutions of Rome. His religious policy was inspired by the Nymph Egeria who came at night to give him advice in the grotto of the Camenae near a sacred spring. The institution of a calender based on the phases of the moon, and the distinction between *dies fasti* and *dies refasti* were attributed to him, along with many other cultural attributions. Numa possessed magic powers such as the ability to create sumptuous dishes from nothing, and was given the credit for persuading JUPITER to content himself with turning thunder aside with onion heads, instead of the heads of men. He died at an extremely great age and was buried on the right bank of the river Tiber on the Janiculum.

NUN

In Egyptian mythology the personification of primeval watery chaos. His title of 'father of the gods' refers to this original existence as the substance out of which creation began. However once ATUM emerged spontaneously out of Nun to create the cosmos, Nun had no further role to play. The concept of Nun as the primeval matter is preserved in temple complexes where the sacred lake served both to symbolize Nun and to provide a practical service to the priests for ritual ablutions.

Below Neptune and Amphitrite are removed from their marine setting in this mosaic from the Nymphaeum of a house in the Roman town of Pompeii. The excellent preservation of much of Pompeii is due to its interment under layers of lava and ash when the volcano Vesuvius erupted in AD 79.

Left above The Egyptian sky goddess Nut arches above the body of her brother the earth god Geb; the painting is from the *Papyrus of Tameniu*, 21st dynasty.

Left below This glazed figure of a sow with its piglets dates from about 600 BC; the sow was sacred to Nut.

Below Detail from the wooden shabti-box of Anhai, a musician priestess of Amun, dating from about 1000 BC. Anhai and her soul, represented by the bird, are shown receiving water from Nut in her aspect as nurturing goddess of the sycamore tree.

NUT

An Egyptian cosmic godddess representing the vault of the sky, daughter of the air god SHU and moisture goddess TEFNUT. Her consort is her brother the earth god GEB, above whose prone body she arches her own, her hands and feet each at one of the four cardinal points. Although depicted as separated from Geb by the air god Shu, her sexual union with the earth god resulted in the four children who form the link between the cosmic deities and the throne of Egypt – OSIRIS, ISIS, SETH and NEPHTHYS. In the tomb of Sety I (1306-1290 BC) in the Valley of the Kings, Nut is shown as the great celestial cow with the sun god sailing across the underside of her body. The strength of Nut prevented the ungovernable forces of chaos from devastating Egypt. Her relationship with the sun god is a fascinating contradiction. In the theogony of Heliopolis she is the granddaughter of the sun god RE but one explanation of his nightly disappearance is that Nut swallowed him to give birth to the sun again at dawn.

ODIN

The chief Viking god, equivalent to the Norse Woden. He was, in the broad sense, father of gods and men and was called Allfather. He had many other names and nicknames (said to be 116), generally relating to different aspects of his doings. Although he was to all intents and purposes the parallel to the classical ZEUS and JUPITER, he was actually equated with MERCURY in the classical world – the link apparently being in their both being leaders of souls.

Odin's wife was FREYA (Frigg) by whom he produced the Aesir race, the Norse gods; his sons were BALDER, HEIMDALL, Hermod, HODER, TYR and Vidarr (Vali). He was an all-seeing and wise god, who acquired these attributes by various stratagems. To learn the secrets of the runes of wisdom he had himself hung upon the Ash Tree; in another version he acquired wisdom from a drink from Mimir's Well for which he paid with one of his eyes. He knew all that happened in the world, since he sat brooding with two ravens, Huginn and Muninn, on his shoulders, on the watch-tower Hlidskjalf. Each dawn he sent the ravens off to circle the world and bring him news before breakfast.

There are many descriptions of Odin in his various disguises, the principal one being as an old bent man with one eye and wearing a deep slouch hat. Among his magic possessions three were pre-eminent: the eight-legged stallion Sleipnir, his magic spear Gungnir and his gold ring Draupnir. The latter two items were made by the dwarves Brokkr and Sindri. Gungnir, once started on a thrust, could not be stopped and Draupnir dropped eight similar gold rings every ninth night.

Because of his all-seeing wisdom Odin knew that the death of Balder would presage Ragnarok, the Doom of the Gods, and there was nothing he

Far left The craggy height of Mount Olympus rises over a mile and a half into the sky. In ancient times it was supposed to touch heaven with its top, and so was called the home of the Greek gods. Wind, rain and clouds never approached; on Mount Olympus it was perpetual spring.

Above Sixth century AD Germanic gold coin from a hoard in Denmark. The design is based on a Roman coin, but the rider god featured is probably Odin, lord of the Norse gods.

Left This richly decorated stela from Sweden shows scenes from Norse mythology, including Odin riding his eight-legged horse Sleipnir on which he fought in the last battle of the gods, the Ragnarok.

Right Tenth century cross-slab found in the Isle of Man which curiously combines Christian and pagan symbolism. The cross is decorated with Viking carving and beside it is shown Odin, with his raven and spear, being attacked by the wolf Fenrir at Ragnarok, the last battle of the gods. Perhaps it symbolizes the defeat of paganism by the shining force of Christianity.

Below The Norse gods Odin, Thor and Freyr are portrayed on this twelfth century Swedish wallhanging.

could do about it once events were set in motion. He attempted to stave off the crisis by chaining the wolf FENRIR and also LOKI, thrusting Jormungandr the World Serpent into the Sea and Loki's daughter Hel into Niflheim (the Underworld), but all to no avail. He knew that the gods must be defeated in the last battle. Loki and Surt (another fire aspect) led all the forces of evil, fire giants, frost giants, mountain giants and Hel with her Underworld dead, against the gods in Asgard. Odin knew that his own death would come about by being devoured by the wolf Fenrir. At least he is avenged by his son Vidarr who leaps forward and, planting his foot in the wolf's lower jaw, levers his upper jaw open until the jaws rip apart and the beast dies. At the last, the fires of Surt scourge across the earth and burn up the gods and heaven – for the moment, the fire (i.e. Loki) is triumphant but not for long, because there arises a new heaven and a new earth that finds its parallels in the Revelation of St John. It is peopled by two humans, Lif and Lifthrasir, who have survived by hiding in Hoddmimir's wood.

ODYSSEUS

The most famous hero of all antiquity. The Latin form is Ulysses. He was the son of Laertes, king of Ithaca and Anticlea. Odysseus was one of the suitors for the hand of HELEN, and so when she was carried off to Troy by PARIS, Odysseus was bound, like all the other suitors, to help rescue her. Although he feigned madness in order to escape his obligations to Helen's father (which was particularly ironic in that he was the originator of the oath of mutual help), he is subsequently portrayed in Homer's *Odyssey* and, in particular, in the *Iliad* as not only cunning and energetic but also as good in counsel as in battle.

Odysseus played an important part in many of the key events of the Trojan War, particularly in missions involving either diplomacy, oratory or espionage. Thus it was he who was placed in charge of the mission to ACHILLES when AGAMEMNON wanted a reconciliation with the latter. Odysseus is credited with the idea of building the Wooden Horse and was the first to leap out of it when he accompanied MENELAUS on his mission to seize Helen. After the death of Achilles a quarrel arose between AJAX, son of Telamon, and Odysseus in the contest for the dead hero's armor. The power of his oratory persuaded the army that Odysseus was most deserving of this honor since it was he who had served the Greek cause best.

Later, on his way home from Troy, Odysseus was held prisoner by the Cyclops, a one-eyed giant, but he was able to escape under the belly of a ram when the Cyclops became drunk on the wine which he had brought as a token of friendship. Odysseus then reached the island of Aeolus, the Warden of the Winds, where he was given a bag containing all the winds except the one necessary to blow him straight back to Ithaca. He and his companions were within sight of the fires of the shepherds on Ithaca when he fell asleep; one of his companions opened the bag and they were all blown back to King Aeolus again. After many more adventures, including a shipwreck in which all his companions died, Odysseus returned to Ithaca, showered with gifts from Alcinous, some 20 years since his departure for Troy.

PENELOPE, Odysseus' wife, was waiting for him, resisting the demands of 108 suitors by saying that she would give one of them an answer once she had finished weaving a shroud for old Laertes. This she wove by day and unpicked by night. Odysseus returned to the palace dressed as a beggar and, although he spoke to Penelope, he withheld his identity from her. For her part, she had arranged an archery competition between the suitors for the next day, the winner of which would win her hand. The competitors would use

Odysseus' own bow. When it transpired that not one of the 108 suitors could bend it, Odysseus was handed the bow. He accomplished the task at the first shot, going on to kill the suitors. Odysseus at last revealed himself to Penelope, removing any lingering doubts by describing secrets of the nuptial chamber known only to themselves. The next day, Odysseus went to the country where his father lived and presented himself to him. He then went on to appease his last enemy, the god POSEIDON, by founding a shrine in his honor.

Top Odysseus with his crew passes the sirens' rock unharmed. The sirens sang so sweetly that anyone who heard them could not help but approach and be drowned in the dangerous tides, but the ingenious Odysseus had himself tied to the mast and so became the first man to hear the sirens and survive.

Above This Greek red-figure vase shows the sirens as having the bodies of vultures and the heads of women.

Right Oedipus answers the riddle set by the sphinx and so frees Thebes from a curse and sets in train his own destruction. The sphinx asked him what creature goes on four legs in the morning, two at noon and three in the evening. The answer is man, who crawls in infancy, walks in maturity, but needs a stick in old age.

OEDIPUS

The hero of one of the best known legends in Greek literature, given to us by Sophocles, Aeschylus and Euripedes. Laius, king of Thebes, was warned by an oracle that if ever he had a son, that son would not only kill him but bring a terrible succession of misfortunes upon his house. To avert this, when Laius fathered Oedipus by Jocasta, he had the boy left on a hillside exposed to the elements, intending his death. To assist this plan he had Oedipus' ankles pierced so as to join them together with a strap. However, the boy was found by Corinthian shepherds, who happened to be in the area. They took him home to their king, Polybus, whom they knew to be childless and in need of an heir.

Oedipus was brought up at the court of Polybus until (in the story presented by the tragedians) one day it was revealed to him that he was in reality only the adoptive son of Polybus. Oedipus set off to consult the Delphic oracle as to the true identity of his parents. On his way there he was insulted by King Laius' herald, Polyphontes. In his anger he slew both the herald and his own father. Frightened by what he had done, Oedipus proceeded to Thebes. There he met the Sphinx and successfully guessed her riddle. In so doing not only did he bring about the death of the Sphinx, but he also freed the Thebans from its curse. In their gratitude they gave him the hand of Laius' widow (his own mother) and made him king.

Soon, however, the secret of Oedipus' birth came to be revealed. In early versions of the story this is because of the scars on his ankles inflicted by Laius on the young Oedipus. Sophocles later built his tragedy around the inexorable revelation of the facts. A plague ravaged Thebes and would not cease until Laius' death was avenged. Oedipus pronounced a curse on the murderer, asking Tiresias the identity of the guilty man. Tiresias did not dare to give an answer and was immediately suspected of the murder. His supposed untrustworthiness was further demonstrated when Jocasta cited what she thought was Tiresias' false prophecy concerning the death of Laius. For surely he was killed not by his son but by brigands at a crossroads? Oedipus was soon seized by a terrible suspicion, which was confirmed when messengers from Corinth informed him that Polybus was dead and that he should go to Corinth, take the throne and marry the queen. This would not be incestuous, they said, because he was a foundling. The account given of the finding of the child left no room for doubt: Oedipus had killed his own father and committed incest with Jocasta.

She fled into the palace and killed herself, and Oedipus then blinded himself, falling victim to his own curse. He died in the village of Colonus after long and painful travels.

ONURIS

Egyptian bearded spear-carrying god with a crown of four plumes, a warrior and hunter with his most important sanctuary near Abydos at the ancient city of This. The etymology of his name means 'He who brings back the far-off one'; in order to gain a consort he pursued Mekhit, a lioness goddess into Nubia, captured her and brought her back into Egypt. His prowess as a hunter gave him the reputation of slaughterer of the enemies of the sun god.

ORESTES

A son of AGAMEMNON and CLYTEMNESTRA. Mentioned only briefly by Homer and Hesiod, he was the last major figure of Greek tragedy, his story being told by Aeschylus, Sophocles and Euripedes. The myth has many different versions, but all agree that Orestes was motivated by the desire to avenge the death of his father, Agamemnon, who had been assassinated upon his return from Troy by Clytemnestra and her lover, Aegisthus. Orestes himself was threatened by his mother's dagger when his sister, ELECTRA, spirited him away to be brought up in the home of Strophus, Orestes' uncle by marriage.

When he reached manhood, APOLLO ordered Orestes to avenge his father's death by killing Aegisthus and Clytemnestra. To effect this, Orestes presented himself to Clytemnestra in the guise of a traveler bearing news (of his own death). Thinking herself free from retribution for the murder of Orestes' father, Clytemnestra sent for Aegisthus, whereupon Orestes murdered them both. However, despite its divine sanction, Orestes was tormented by the FURIES for this deed. Driven mad, he was tried at Athens for patricide and acquitted, but could not regain his sanity until he had stolen the wooden statue of Artemis which was in the land of the Taurians. These people sacrificed all foreigners that they found in the land. Orestes and his life-long companion Pylades, son of Strophus, were captured upon landing in Tauris but the priestess of Artemis, IPHIGENIA, turned out to be none other than Orestes' eldest sister. They all escaped together with the statue, Orestes going on to become the most powerful monarch in the Peloponnesus.

Above Orpheus with his magical music charms the animals on this sixteenth century Italian plate – including a dragon and a unicorn as well as more mundane creatures.

ORPHEUS

The myth of Orpheus is one of the most obscure and certainly the most symbolic in Greek mythology. Traces of it can be found at a very early date and it later developed into a full scale theology with its own literature. Indeed the myth had a certain influence upon early Christian belief and iconography. While it is generally accepted that his father was Oeagrus, the identity of Orpheus' mother is more problematical. It is usually given as Calliope, chief of the nine Muses. There are three main legends concerning Orpheus. These concern his role on the expedition of the ARGONAUTS, his descent into the Underworld and the reasons for and the circumstances surrounding his death.

Orpheus' role on the expedition of the Argonauts to Iolcus in pursuit of the Golden Fleece (see JASON) was an important one, for although weaker than the other heroes – acting as a coxswain instead of as an oarsman – he used his voice to great effect. Thus he stilled the waves during a storm and later saved the Argonauts from seduction by the Sirens by singing with even greater sweetness than they.

The descent of Orpheus into the Underworld

was a theme developed mainly in the Alexandrian period. Walking beside a river in Thrace EURYD-ICE, Orpheus' wife, was pursued by Aristeus. As she fled from her pursuer she was fatally bitten by a serpent. Inconsolable at her tragic death, Orpheus went down to the Underworld to find her. With the music of his lyre he charmed not only the monsters of Hades but even the Underworld gods. Indeed the poets strive to outdo each other in their imaginative descriptions of this divine music: Ixion's wheel ceased to turn, Sisyphus' stone remained poised without support, Tantalus forgot his perpetual thirst and even the Danaides forgot about trying to fill their seive. HADES and PERSEPHONE agreed to restore Eurydice to her husband but on one condition: Orpheus must not look back at her until he reached the world of light outside the Underworld. Orpheus had almost achieved this when, for some reason, he looked back. Eurydice became as a shadow and when Orpheus tried to follow the specter back into the Underworld, he was refused admission by the ferryman, CHARON. Only the sound of his lyre in grottos or mountains could soothe his grief.

The death of Orpheus has given rise to a number of traditions. While in most legends he is killed by the Ciconian women of Thrace, their motive is unclear. Did they resent his fidelity to the memory of Eurydice? Did he surround himself with young men? Or did he institute mysteries based on his experiences in the Underworld, and restricted to men only, of which they were jealous? After his death, the Muses gathered up the pieces of his body and buried them. The head and lyre being missing, they were buried separately at Lesbos and the Lesbians were rewarded with the abiity to make fine music. The lyre later rose to the sky as the constellation Lyra. Orpheus' soul was taken to the Elysian Fields where it continued to sing for the benefit of the blessed ones. As a Thracian, Orpheus is often depicted singing with his lyre in Thracian dress in the region of Olympus.

Right This Roman mosaic shows Orpheus with a rather more authentic lyre, together with a centaur and a satyr playing his flute.

OSIRIS

Egyptian deity, probably always first and foremost a god of death or the Underworld, but legends of an existence above ground became added to his myth in order to explain the eternal cycle of life and death. His appearance in the Egyptian pantheon is not archaeologically provable before about 2400 BC, which is later than other major deities such as HORUS and SETH. Osiris was the eldest of the offspring of GEB and NUT who inherited the throne of Egypt. In pharaonic sources such as the Pyramid Texts, statue and temple reliefs, the reign of Osiris and his sister-wife ISIS is brought to an end in a murderous assault by his brother, the god Seth. The goddess Isis found her husband's body and used her magical power to hold back the putrefaction of his flesh. The god THOTH helped embalm Osiris and ANUBIS presided over the ritual. Through the skills and magic of Isis the phallus of Osiris was stimulated and the goddess was able to become pregnant with the seed of her murdered consort. Osiris then vanished from the stage of Egypt to become ruler of the Underworld, leaving Isis pregnant with his son HORUS who would avenge his murder and regain the throne from Seth.

According to the Greek author Plutarch, writing in the first century AD, Osiris cured Egypt of living in barbarism by introducing agriculture and laws. However he incurred the jealousy of his brother Seth (Typhon in Plutarch) who plotted to gain the throne. He devised a scheme whereby at a banquet he would offer as a prize an exquisitely inlaid chest to whomsoever could fit exactly into it; of course it was made to fit the measurements of Osiris alone. Osiris – fairly gullible for a god in Plutarch – gets into the chest, the lid is thrown shut upon him and the chest is then hurled into the river Nile. It is carried from the eastern Delta into the Mediterranean sea and tossed upon the shore of Byblos in the Lebanon. There a tree grows around it which is then felled to become a column in the palace of the prince of Byblos. Isis pursues the route to Byblos. She disguises herself and sits on the shore attracting the attention of the handmaids of the Queen of Byblos whom she covers with aromatic perfume. The Queen is enchanted by the scent and urges the handmaids to bring the woman to the palace. Isis becomes nurse to the Queen's baby son. For some reason she secretly decides to make the young prince immortal by setting his cradle on fire at night, turning herself into a sparrow-hawk and flying around the room. When the Queen of Byblos disturbs this magical procedure by entering the room unexpectedly and falling into hysteria at what she sees, the spell is broken. Isis then demands Osiris' body from the palace column and returns to

Egypt. The whole Byblos episode seems to relate to the extensive trade in cedar, juniper and pine between Egypt and the Lebanon, from the third millennium BC down to about 1000 BC. Isis took care of Osiris' body in the Delta marshes but one day neglected it – the very time when Seth was out hunting. He cut Osiris's body into 14 parts and scattered them throughout the Nile valley. Isis recovered all the limbs of Osiris but had to fashion a sexual organ for the god since his phallus was thrown in the Nile and swallowed by fish. Eventually however Seth is vanquished and Horus victoriously ascends the throne of Osiris.

Above Osiris in his full regalia as god of the Underworld. From a Theban tomb wall-painting.

PAN

Greek god of flocks and shepherds, worshiped widely in Greece after the fifth century BC, with sacrifices of cows, rams, milk and honey made at his sanctuaries and temples. He lived in Arcadia in a grotto and spent his time chasing nymphs and dancing. During the hottest part of the day he would sleep and during the night he caused 'panic' terror for those walking through the forests. In some versions he is the child of Zeus and the nymph Callisto, in others Hermes is his father, having seduced PENELOPE (later married to ODYSSEUS) in goat form while she tended her father Icarius's flocks on Mount Taygetus. Pan was goat-like in appearance although standing on his hind legs. He was known particularly for his sexual energy, having love affairs with ECHO and DIANA among others, as well as with boys. He instructed APOLLO in prophecy and taught Daphnis how to play the syrinx or shepherd's pipe, which he himself had invented. Pan's birth story is recounted in a Homeric hymn but he is most evidenced by artists, in vase paintings and sculpture. He was particularly favored among the Egyptians and was worshiped there with the greatest solemnity as an emblem of fecundity.

The name Pan in Greek means 'all' and in later antiquity Pan came to personify the universe and indeed to represent the whole of paganism itself, while retaining his rustic element. In Roman times Pan was identified with the woodland god Faunus.

PANDORA

The first woman on earth, she plays an important part in numerous versions of the Greek creation myth. Her name means 'all gifts' and reflects her story. When PROMETHEUS stole fire from the forge of HEPHAESTUS to warm mankind, ZEUS was angry and ordered Hephaestus to make a woman out of earth who, with her charm and beauty, would bring misery to all humans. APOLLO gave this woman beauty, HERMES gave her cunning and boldness and took her to Epimetheus, Prometheus' brother, who instantly forgot his brother's advice to reject gifts from Zeus. Thus began man's misery.

The story of Pandora's 'box' gives a further explanation of human misery: curious at what might be inside a large earthenware pot, Pandora lifted the lid. Alas, it was Epimetheus' pot, containing all the evils in the world and just one good, namely hope; when the lid was removed, all the evils escaped, leaving just hope at the bottom.

Far left The Portland Vase, one of the most famous and precious survivals from the Roman era, shows the sea-nymph Thetis, mother of Achilles, reclining on a rock, flanked by Aphrodite and Mercury, two of Achilles' protectors. The vase is made of glass and dates from the first century AD.

Above Pan, the Greek god of flocks and shepherds, together with a satyr, detail from a Roman sarcophagus.

Left Pan, here shown as a bearded, goatlike creature, plays knucklebones with Aphrodite.

PARIS

In Greek legend the son of PRIAM, who was exposed at birth because his mother, Hecuba, had dreamt when pregnant that she would produce a torch issuing serpents. Shepherds found him and brought him up, and his identity was revealed at funeral games in Troy, when the prize was to be a bull of which Paris was particularly fond. The games were being held for Paris himself, in commemoration of the son who died so young. Paris won all the events but one of his brothers was jealous and tried to kill him, so he took refuge at the altar of Zeus and there was recognized by his sister CASSANDRA, who took him back to the palace.

While living as a shepherd on Mount Ida, Paris was present at a contest in which the beauties of ATHENA, HERA and APHRODITE were being compared. No-one wanted to judge who should win the prize of a golden apple, and so Paris was selected to make the decision. Athena promised wisdom and victory, Hera would make him ruler of all Asia, but he chose Aphrodite who offered the love of the most beautiful woman in the world, HELEN of Sparta. This choice made, Paris abandoned his nymph lover Oenone and, in spite of warnings of future dangers, went to Sparta with AENEAS. There they were welcomed by MENELAUS, Helen's husband, who then departed on a journey leaving Helen to entertain the guests.

Paris wooed and won Helen's love with his charming nature and good looks and took her back with him to Troy. During the Trojan War that followed, Paris was defeated early on by Menelaus but was rescued by Aphrodite. He helped to kill ACHILLES, shooting an arrow at his heel.

Paris' story bears heavily on the whole mythology of Greece, focusing on the choice of Aphrodite which set in train the events of the Trojan War.

PASIPHAE

In Greek myth the wife of MINOS, king of Crete, and mother of ARIADNE and the MINOTAUR. She was the sister of CIRCE and shared some of her ability in sorcery. When Pasiphae's husband Minos prayed to POSEIDON to send a bull as a sign of approval of Minos' rule of Crete, the god sent a white bull and then caused Pasiphae to develop a passion for it. This may have been to punish Pasiphae for despising the cult of Aphrodite. Burning with passion for the bull, Pasiphae persuaded DAEDALUS to create a lifelike heifer and in this guise she seduced the bull. The result of this union was the creature, half man and half bull, known as the Minotaur. Pasiphae was jealous of her husband's love affairs and put a spell on him so that any woman he made love to was devoured by serpents coming out of his body.

Below left Fine second century AD mosaic from Antioch in Syria showing the perplexity of the young shepherd Paris when asked to judge between three goddesses. The Trojan War resulted from his judgment, for he chose Aphrodite, goddess of love, who promised him the most beautiful human, Helen of Sparta, as his wife.

Below right Daedalus shows the impatient Pasiphae the wooden cow he has made in which she can seduce the bull of Minos, from a Roman wall painting at Pompeii.

Left The wounded Patroclus is tenderly bandaged by his friend and companion Achilles. When Achilles refused to continue fighting in the Trojan War because of a dispute with Agamemnon, Patroclus borrowed his armor to encourage the Greeks, but was killed by Hector. Achilles sallied out in vengeance and in turn killed Hector.

PATROCLUS PEGASUS

The companion of the Greek hero ACHILLES. He was the son of Menoetius of Opus, but was taken away to be brought up with Achilles at Pythia after he accidentally killed a friend during a game of dice. Patroclus went to Troy to be with Achilles but ended up taking a crucial part in the fighting. He withdrew from battle when Achilles withdrew but then borrowed his friend's armor to fight. He killed many Trojans but was himself killed by HECTOR. Achilles was deeply saddened by the loss of Patroclus and returned to the battle determined to avenge his death. Patroclus' body was burnt and the ashes buried in a mound where Achilles was also eventually buried. The funeral and games held in his honor are described in detail in Book 23 of Homer's *Iliad*.

The winged horse of the gods of the Greeks and of the Muses, born from the head of MEDUSA when it was severed by PERSEUS or, in other version, fathered on her by POSEIDON. Pegasus went up to Olympus and carried thunder and lightning for ZEUS.

He was caught by BELLEROPHON at a well with a special golden bridle, but when Bellerophon became too proud of his conquest of the Chimaera and the Amazons and tried to ride up to heaven, Pegasus, stung by a fly sent from Zeus, threw him off. The inspiration of the Muses came from the spring called Hippocrene on Mount Helicon, which first flowed when Pegasus kicked the ground with his hoof. Pegasus eventually became a constellation.

Above Persephone returns from the Underworld where she has been held captive by Hades. Old men rejoice and the earth springs into flower on this bronze Etruscan vessel.

Far right The Cyclops Polyphemus is blinded by Odysseus and his men, as shown on a sixth century BC Greek wine jar.

PERSEPHONE

The daughter of DEMETER and ZEUS, who was worshiped with her mother as goddess of vegetation and growth. The story of her abduction represents an attempt by the ancients to explain how the seed lies dormant underground for part of the year and then springs forth, restored to life. Persephone was snatched away while picking flowers by HADES, who took her down to the Underworld. Her mother searched all over the world to find Persephone but had no luck until in Sicily she reached the River Cyane, where Hades made his descent into his kingdom. Demeter blamed the land for swallowing up her daughter but was persuaded to ask the help of ZEUS. This was granted on condition that Persephone should have eaten nothing during her time with Hades, but when Demeter descended to the Underworld she found that Persephone had been tempted by the god and eaten a pomegranate. A compromise was struck, whereby Persephone spent half the year in the Underworld with Hades and half on earth with Demeter. The story was taken over by the Romans and assimilated into their Proserpina.

PERSEUS

A mythological Greek hero from Argos and the son of ZEUS and DANAE, famed for cutting off the head of MEDUSA. Perseus' grandfather, Acrisius, was afraid of a prophecy that if Danae had a son the son would kill him, so he set Danae and the baby Perseus adrift on the sea in a box. They came to shore at the island of Seriphos and were taken in by a fisherman, Dictys, whose brother was Polydectes, ruler of Seriphos. Polydectes fell in love with Danae and, when he found that Perseus guarded his mother well, sent him on a quest to bring back the head of Medusa the GORGON.

On his way Perseus was helped by HERMES and ATHENA, while the Nymphs lent him winged sandals and the helmet of HADES, which made him invisible. Thus he avoided being turned into stone by the Gorgon's glance while he cut off her head. From her neck sprang a giant, Chrysaor, and the winged horse Pegasus. Taking the head, Perseus set off home but in Ethiopia he fell in love with ANDROMEDA, who had been offered as a sacrifice on a rock. He used Medusa's head to turn the sea monster to stone in order to be able to marry her. Returning to Seriphos with Andromeda, he found that Polydectes had tried to rape Danae and took revenge by turning Polydectes to stone and putting Dictys (Polydectes' brother) in

PENELOPE

The faithful wife of ODYSSEUS, by whom she had one son, Telemachus. Her husband was reluctant to go to Troy because he did not want to be separated from her. During Odysseus' absence, many suitors came to woo Penelope but she steadfastly refused, maintaining that she had to finish weaving a shroud for her aged father-in-law Laertes before she chose between them. By day she sat weaving and by night she unpicked each day's work so that it was never completed. This ruse was uncovered by Penelope's slaves and she had to finish off the shroud, but still managed to fend off the suitors. When Odysseus returned after 20 years, she recognized him by his strength as he was the only one who could bend the bow of Odysseus. After Odysseus' death she married Telegonus. In later versions, however, Penelope was far from the perfect wife but an evil creature, who slept with each of the suitors in turn and conceived PAN.

charge of Seriphos. Athena took the head of Medusa and put it in the centre of her shield.

Perseus wanted to see his grandfather again so he went back to Argos, but Acrisius was still afraid of the oracle's warning and fled. The two were both present at funeral games in Pelasgia, however, and Perseus, taking part in the games, accidentally killed his grandfather with a discus. This terrible fulfilment of the oracle's prophecy left Perseus unable to claim his grandfather's kingdom so he swapped with his cousin Megapenthes, who became king of Argos, and he himself became king of Tiryns.

PLUTO

The name used in Greek and Roman mythology to describe HADES, the god of the Underworld, and means 'the rich'. It reflects the rich mineral resources beneath the ground and the rich earth above it. In art he is shown with the horn of plenty. Pluto is rarely mentioned in myths, possibly because it was thought to be bad luck to say his name. Other names associated with Pluto include Orcus and Dis Pater (Father of Riches). ZEUS (JUPITER) apparently took over Pluto's sphere of power, as he did from POSEIDON, because with Zeus as the single most powerful diety others lost influence. There was a temple to Pluto at Byzantium.

POLLUX see DIOSCURI

POLYPHEMUS

In Greek myth a Cyclops (one-eyed giant) and son of POSEIDON. He reared sheep and goats, probably in Sicily. In one story he was the lover of a beautiful nymph called Galatea but was jilted for being too boorish. In the *Odyssey* Polyphemus finds ODYSSEUS and his men hiding in his cave and eats some of them. They are still trapped in the cave the same evening so Odysseus makes the Cyclops drunk with strong wine and blinds him by poking out his one eye with a stake. When Polyphemus cried out for help, no one came, as he said that 'no man' was killing him: Odysseus had tricked him, saying that his name was 'no man'.

When Odysseus and his men escaped Polyphemus threw rocks at them, almost destroying their ship.

Below The hero Perseus kills the Gorgon.

POSEIDON

One of the Olympian dieties of the Greeks, the son of CRONUS and RHEA. His sphere of power covered the sea, water (not rivers) and earth-quakes. He had similar powers to ZEUS in these special fields, but was ultimately less powerful than his brother. He was worshiped most on the mythical island of Atlantis, having failed to gain Athens, Argos and other more central areas. Offerings were made on occasions when naviga-tion and a calm voyage were needed. He was also worshiped in connection with horses, probably because he was introduced to Greece by the Indo-European traders who also introduced horses. Poseidon's consort was Amphitrite but he also had affairs with MEDUSA, by whom in one version he was father of PEGASUS, and with DEM-ETER.

Poseidon played an important part in the Tro-jan War. He built the walls of Troy with APOLLO but was cheated of his pay so sent a sea-monster to scourge the land. This made him hostile to the Trojans and he actively helped the Greeks, taking on the appearance of Calchas to encourage them. His participation was curtailed by Zeus, but he saved AENEAS when ACHILLES was just about to kill him.

Above   This magnificent bronze statue, one of the masterpieces of Greek classical sculpture, was found in the sea and is thought to represent Poseidon hurling his trident.

Right   The temple of Poseidon at Sounion, mainland Greece, stands on a high promontory looking out over the sea god's kingdom.

PRIAM

King of Troy during the Trojan War. He was the youngest son of Laomedon. In his youth he fought the Amazons, but by the time of the Trojan War he was too old to fight and so he presided over councils and was widely respected, even by his enemies and most of the gods, for his wisdom. It was his youngest son PARIS who was responsible for provoking the Trojan war by carrying off HELEN, wife of MENELAUS of Sparta. Priam countenanced the abduction by receiving Helen in Troy. His son HECTOR played a leading role in the fighting and on his death Priam offered a huge ransom for Hector's body and persuaded ACHILLES to part with it; the king's sadness and desperation at seeing his sons die is well illustrated in Book 24 of the *Iliad*. His wife Hecuba, mother of his many children, stood by him throughout the war but, when Priam insisted on taking up arms to save his burning city, Hecuba persuaded him to take refuge at the altar of Zeus. This led to Priam's death; first he was forced to watch his son Polites die at the sword of Neoptolemus, Achilles' son, and then he himself was slain by Neoptolemus. Priam's death was mourned by Hecuba but his body remained unburied. His name became synonomous with mixed fortunes.

Above The aged Priam, king of Troy, kneels to kiss the hand of Achilles, supplicating the return of his son Hector's body. Achilles was touched by the old man's tears and restored his son's body for proper burial, allowing a truce of twelve days in which the funeral rites could be observed.

Left Roman bronze showing Poseidon holding a horse's head.

Right Terracotta statue from the
second century BC showing Psyche
winged, as the consort of Cupid, after
she has earned the right to divinity by
her devotion and perseverance.

PRIAPUS

PROMETHEUS

The Greek god of fertility, born with a massively enlarged phallus which was his symbol. His phallus could ward off the evil eye, so statues of him in gardens acted as scarecrows. He was the son of APHRODITE, but HERA, jealous of Aphrodite's beauty, made him deformed from birth. His mother rejected him and so he was brought up in the country. In some stories Priapus was the son of DIONYSUS; certainly his cult was similar to Dionysus' and he was often shown as an ass because during a Dionysiac festival he was disturbed by the braying of an ass while trying to seduce a nymph. This story highlights the mix of lust and stupidity for which he was known.

A Greek demi-god, one of the race of Titans. He created man from clay and was thus seen as the master craftsman. Prometheus used his natural wiles to steal fire from Olympus for man, as Zeus had hidden it. Having brought fire to earth, he was unable to make a spark from rubbing wood so he stole a smoldering fennel stalk and this time got a fire going for man. Zeus was again duped by Prometheus when faced with the choice of sacrificial offerings. He chose the larger portion, containing all the fat and the bones of the victim, leaving the smaller but more valuable portion for men. Punishment for these tricks came when Zeus brought misery to all mankind in the shape of PANDORA, and chained Prometheus to a rock with an eagle sent each day to peck out his liver; as he was immortal, his liver grew back to its full size each night. Prometheus was eventually released by HERACLES and took on immortality from CHIRON, who wished to lose his immortality and die. In addition to his trickery Prometheus was also known for his prophetic powers; his son Deucalion was warned by him of the imminent flood.

PSYCHE

Means 'soul' in Greek. From the earliest times it was accepted that the soul was separate from the body as its 'double'. Later the soul was considered to be like a winged spirit that departed from the body at death. All such winged souls were female, and from the fifth century BC onwards they were shown as butterflies. The story of the mythological character Psyche served to elaborate the theory.

Psyche was a most beautiful princess with no suitors, as everyone feared her beauty. Her father, on consulting an oracle, was told to dress her up for marriage and leave her on a rock, from which she would be taken by a monster. This was done, with accompanying funerary honors, and the girl was wafted away by the wind. Landing in a valley, she slept then woke opposite a big palace. Voices guided her in and stayed with her every day, while she had the company of her monster husband each night. She never saw him; if she did, she was told she would lose him for ever. After some weeks Psyche missed her family so much that she persuaded the monster to let her go back for a while, but when she returned home her sisters teased her with the fact that she had never seen her husband. They persuaded her to look at him one night: she discovered that he was a most handsome youth, namely Love (EROS, CUPID) himself, but he awoke and fled. Left alone, Psyche wandered the earth, but APHRODITE, who was jealous of Psyche's beauty, imprisoned her and set her menial tasks. Her last task for Aphrodite was to go down to the Underworld to fetch a flask of the water of youth, but on her way back she opened it and fell into a deep sleep. While she was asleep, Eros saw her and woke her, and asked permission to marry her. Zeus agreed, and Aphrodite was at last reconciled with her rival.

PTAH

Egyptian creator and craftsman god of Memphis which had become the political and administra-tive capital of Egypt following the unification of the northern and southern kingdoms around 3000 BC. He is represented anthropomorphically in a tight fitting linen wrap. A basalt slab in the British Museum known as the Shabaka Stone shows Ptah, who had a manifestation also as Tatenen (or the 'risen land') creating the cosmos in a purely metaphysical way. This represents the earliest example of the 'logos doctrine' yet discovered; the god, who was self created, conceived the idea of the universe in his heart and spoke it into existence through his tongue. This account of the creation of the world by Ptah ranks as one of the greatest intellectual achievements of the Ancient World. Ptah's temple at Memphis, hardly surviving today except in some colossal New Kingdom statuary, was one of the most impressive in Egypt. Ptah was worshiped there with his consort the lioness SAKHMET.

Below Bronze and gilt statue of the Egyptian creator god Ptah, wearing his characteristic linen wrap.

RE

Egyptian sun god of Heliopolis, the supreme tran-
scendental deity manifest in the three spheres of
Sky, Earth and Underworld. Re is really the power
of the sun disk which the Egyptians felt could be
best indicated by a falcon carrying on its head the
sun encircled by the protective cobra-goddess. In
some myths the god Re is seen as an ageing
monarch of the universe whose hair is of lapis
lazuli, whose bones are made of silver and whose
flesh is the most precious metal, gold. The pharaohs of Egypt formulated a way of enhancing
their divinity by forging a link with the sun god.
They promulgated the concept that each pharaoh
was Re's offspring. Pyramids of the layered style
such as that of King Djoser (2630-2611 BC) at Saqqara symbolized a gigantic stairway for the pharaoh to climb into the sky to join his father the sun
god. True pyramids such as those on the Giza pla-
teau represented the rays of the sun god breaking
through the sky. Re as creator god could be visual-
ized as emerging out of the primeval water within
a primordial lotus flower which opened up to reveal the newly born sun god. The tears of the sun
god fell to earth and from them sprang the human
race, described in most elevated texts as 'the
cattle of Re'. At night the sun god traveled in a boat
through the Underworld bringing life and light to
the gods and goddesses there. He was depicted as
a ram-headed god whose distinctive epithet is
'flesh of Re'. Having journeyed the twelve hours
of night through gates and caverns, past lakes of
fire and lethal serpents, the sun god was born
again into the dawn sky.

Far left This well preserved Egyptian
painting on wood from the 20th or
21st dynasties shows a dead soul,
naked, supplicating the falcon-headed
sun god Re. Above Re's head floats the
sun disk.

Left By c. 900 BC, when this silver
statuette overlaid with gold foil was
made, Re had become conflated with
the god Amun.

Below The sun god Re travels
through the Underworld in his solar
boat, before rising again into the
heavens with the dawn.

REMUS

Son of RHEA SILVIA and ZEUS, and twin brother of ROMULUS, mythical founder of Rome. Remus scorned his brother's attempts at making a preliminary boundary for the new city, and was killed by Romulus for this. His legend probably dates from the fourth century BC.

RENENUTET

Below Romulus and Remus with the wolf that nurtured them, on a late Roman altar found in the port of Ostia.

Egyptian cobra goddess, not frequently represented in iconography but important as a protector of royalty. She appears as a woman with a cobra head sometimes suckling a child. Her gaze as a snake overcomes all the enemies of the pharaoh, and her power was harnesed to the idea of ripening the harvest of barley. As 'lady of the threshing floor' she kept predators away from the grain in her form of the dangerous cobra. Renenutet also symbolized the magical power in the linen garments worn by pharaoh and came to be associated with linen provided to protect the mummified corpse in the afterlife.

RHEA SILVIA

Also known as Ilia, was the daughter of Numitor, rightful king of Rome. Rhea Silvia was one of the Vestal Virgins and thus prevented from marrying, but she was secretly loved by MARS and had twins by him, ROMULUS and REMUS. Amulius, who had usurped the throne from his brother, imprisoned her when he realized she was pregnant, but she escaped, dying in childbirth or killed after she had given birth. In another tradition she is the daughter of AENEAS.

ROMULUS

Mythical founder of Rome, and the son of MARS and RHEA SILVIA. The main thread of this much varied story has Romulus and his twin brother REMUS thrown into the River Tiber, then washed ashore and suckled by a she-wolf. They were brought up by the royal herdsman but were eventually recognized. They then overthrew the king of Alba and decided to found a city of their own nearby. The traditional date for the foundation is around 754 BC. Romulus and Remus built their city on the Palatine Hill but Remus kicked down a new wall, for which act Romulus killed him.

Romulus planned the 'Rape of the Sabines' in order to provide wives for his Romans. During ceremonial games at Rome, to which the Sabines had been invited, the Romans carried off the Sabine women. This led to a war, during which the Sabines besieged the Capitol, but the two sides were eventually reconciled. Romulus then disappeared in a thunderstorm, and became the god Quirinius.

The name Rome is taken from Romulus' name, which itself means Roman. The transferring of names (eponyms) betrays the Greek influence on this myth. As a mythical character, Romulus represents the Roman people, and his story is the creation story of Rome itself.

Left This famous statue is known as the Capitoline wolf, because it was found on the Capitol hill in Rome. It is Etruscan, pre-dating the Roman era, but the figures of Romulus and Remus were probably Roman additions.

Left A more primitive version of the Romulus and Remus story, featuring a huge and predatory wolf and a fully grown man.

SAKHMET

Egyptian lioness goddess of Memphis, very familiar in her form of a graceful female body with leonine head superimposed. Her name meant the 'Powerful One' and admirably suited her ferocious nature. The sun disk which she wore on her head emphasized the fact that her immense power derived from her being the daughter of the sun god RE. There is one particular myth attesting to her bloodthirsty character. The sun god Re was suspicious that men were plotting to overthrow his rule, and sent his avenging 'Eye' down to Egypt. This 'Eye of Re' started out as HATHOR but transformed into Sakhmet for the slaughter. Sakhmet sought out and killed men, and drank their blood. At night the sun god wanted to stop the massacre since if the whole human race was destroyed there would be no upkeep or offerings in the temples. He and the other gods swamped the land of Egypt with barley beer dyed red and on the following morning, when Sakhmet descended to Egypt to complete the killing, she drank what she took to be human blood, became intoxicated and forgot her plan to slaughter the remaining men. The Egyptians portrayed her as a goddess able to bring epidemics but also to ward them off. The title 'priest of Sakhmet' was therefore taken by the magician who was present with the physician at difficult cures. At Memphis Sakhmet was seen as the consort of the creator-god PTAH and mother of the divine child of the Memphite triad, the lotus god Nefertum. Her correlation with the goddess MUT of Thebes led to vast numbers of granite statues of Sakhmet being dedicated during the reign of Amentolep III (1391-1353 BC) in Mut's sanctuary at Karnak. In these statues the goddess is seated or standing holding the papyrus sceptre of North (Lower) Egypt.

SARAPIS

A god created in the early Ptolemaic period, shortly after 300 BC, from existing Egyptian and Greek deities to symbolize the synthesis of the two cultures that the new Greek rulers of Egypt hoped would occur. The concept of this hybrid god was entirely evolved at the court of Alexandria and there is no basis at all for the suggestion by the Roman historian Tacitus that the new deity had origins in Asia Minor.

The Sarapeum at Alexandria was regarded as one of the wonders of the ancient world, and drew pilgrims from far and wide in search of

Far left Early sixteenth century woodcut after Durer, showing the satyr family. Satyrs feature widely in classical mythology as rural demigods, with the heads and bodies of men and the legs and hooves of goats, and short horns on the head. They are often shown in the company of the wine god Bacchus, and were also called fauns.

Above The Egyptian lion-headed goddess Sakhmet, one of the most bloodthirsty and ferocious of the Egyptian pantheon.

Left Exquisitely decorated Egyptian pectoral showing the Pharaoh standing between Sakhmet and the creator god Ptah, her consort.

Right Bronze bust of the Alexandrian god Sarapis showing him assimilated with the Greek father god Zeus.

Below The Roman Emperor Hadrian built his villa at Tivoli near Rome in imitation of the sanctuary of Sarapis at Alexandria; this view shows the epistyle at the north end.

miraculous cures from Sarapis in his aspect of healer.

The name Sarapis was formed from the description of the sacred bull of Memphis after its death as OSIRIS, APIS or Osorapis. The attraction of the bull cult of Egypt's political capital before the conquest of Alexander the Great in 332 BC lay in the underlying concept of resurrection after death, combined with the vigor and fertility of the bull.

From the Hellenistic world Sarapis drew upon a number of deities. The Greek king of the gods ZEUS gave the idea of sovereignty, Helios provided the nature of a sun god, DIONYSUS represented fecundity, ASCLEPIUS endowed the new deity with powers of medical healing and HADES connected Sarapis with the notion of the Greek Underworld. The iconography of Sarapis is totally Hellenistic, representing the god as a bearded man with the symbol of agricultural prosperity on his head. Sarapis became the consort of the goddess ISIS in the Mediterranean world, as in the precinct of the foreign gods on the island of Delos.

SARGON OF AKKAD

Historical ruler (c. 2334-2279 BC), founder of the Semitic Old Akkadian dynasty, who united the cities of Mesopotamia for the first time into an effective empire. Sargon, like his descendant Naram Sin (2254-2218 BC), is the subject of a cycle of stories and traditions, but is principally of interest to mythology on account of the so-called *Sargon Legend*. This narrates how Sargon, who was ignorant of his father's identity, was born in secret to a high priestess who placed him in a reed basket sealed with pitch and deposited it in the river. A water-drawer named Aqqi rescued the boy and brought him up, teaching him to be a gardener. The boy later became king. This theme, the so-called '*infant exposure*' motif, has echoes in other literatures of the ancient world, notably the fate of Moses in Exodus II 1-10.

SATURN

An ancient Italian god, identified with the Greek CRONUS and the Near Eastern BAAL, but he also had all the attributes of DEMETER. The worship of Saturn focused strongly on the Saturnalia, or festival of Saturn, held each year at the end of December. This was a happy celebration involving role reversal, where masters took orders from their slaves. From about the fourth century AD these celebrations became assimilated into those of New Year's Day and Christmas. The temple of Saturn, on the Capitoline Hill, was used as a treasury.

Saturn was the god who civilized Italy, teaching cultivation, following on from JANUS. This is reflected in artistic representations which show Saturn with a scythe. With agriculture central to the wealth of Italy, it was natural for him to be regarded as the god of plenty; he ruled over a Golden Age and then suddenly disappeared, in the way of mythical kings.

Above Painted relief from the temple of Seti I showing Seti before the jackal-headed god Anubis.

Right Bronze and gilt statues of the 19th dynasty from Thebes showing Seth with a beaked head.

[8191]

SEMELE

Daughter of Cadmus, king of Thebes in Boeotia, and mother, by ZEUS, of the god DIONYSUS. She was worshiped at Thebes after her death. Semele's affair with Zeus was interrupted by the jealousy of HERA, who persuaded Semele to test her lover's divinity by asking him to appear in his true shape. Zeus had already agreed to do whatever Semele asked of him, so he appeared as a thunderbolt (his true shape) and Semele was struck dead, but her newly conceived son was made immortal by the thunderbolt. Zeus lodged Dionysus in his thigh until he was born. When he was old enough Dionysus went down into Hades to fetch Semele and took her up to be an Olympian goddess. Semele was also loved by ACTAEON, who was punished for rivaling Zeus.

SETH

Egyptian god of great antiquity and power whose nature incorporated elemental forces of chaos. Seth was one of the children of NUT and GEB in the Heliopolitan theogamy but was probably a god of entirely independent origin with strong support in the north-east Delta and in Upper Egypt around his birthplace of Ombos. A brief survey of episodes in Egyptian history shows that he had loyal adherents in the royal family. Seth could equate readily as god of storms and battle with Middle Eastern gods like BAAL or the Hittite storm-god TESHUB. In addition the goddesses ISHTAR and Anat from Syria entered the Egyptian pantheon as wives of Seth.

In the legend of OSIRIS from the Pyramid Age onward Seth was regarded as a murderer and usurper of the throne of Egypt. In the struggle with HORUS he lost his testicles but in revenge deprived Horus of his sight. Although Seth lost the contest to keep the throne of Egypt his strongest ally remained the sun god. RE took him into the solar boat to speak out of the sky in the sound of thunder.

SHAMASH

(Sumerian Utu), the Mesopotamian sun god and god of justice and fair play, and the god chiefly responsible for communication by omens. Regarded as the son of the moon god, SIN, and brother to ISHTAR, Shamash is possessed of a consistently benevolent character in the sources.

His principal cult was located in the cities of Sippar and Larsa, each housing a temple called Ebabbar. Mythologically he was conceived in Mesopotamian thought to cross over the Heavens in a chariot drawn by steeds during the day, traversing the Underworld during the night. A famous cylinder seal shows Shamash emerging in the morning, carrying his characteristic symbol of a saw. According to the GILGAMESH epic this took place at Mount Mashum. While in the Underworld Shamash was considered responsible for the spirits of the dead, and he plays an important role in magic against ghosts and witches. He is appealed to in many prayers and incantations for intercession and justice. His symbol is a four pointed star with wavy lines, in a circle.

SHU

Originally an Egyptian solar divinity who became subordinated as the idea of air or sunlight separating his two offspring, the sky goddess NUT and the earth god GEB, by physically supporting the sky above the earth with his arms or by sailing between the two in a boat. A reference to the 'Bones of Shu' probably describes the clouds in the sky.

Left Sumerian stela showing the two dedicators standing before the symbols representing the gods Shamash, Sin and Nergal.

Below Greek bronze statue of the sea monster Scylla. During the wanderings of Odysseus, one of the dangers he had to negotiate was the strait between the rock on which Scylla sat and the whirlpool Charybdis, thought to lie between Italy and Sicily.

Right These Viking warriors with their boar's head helmets decorate a bronze matrix used in eighth century Sweden for making decorative plaques for helmets. Sigurd may have worn something similar.

Right The hero Sigurd kills the dragon Fafnir with his potent sword Gram; detail from a wooden door in a twelfth century Norwegian church.

SIGURD

Norse hero, one of the chosen of Odin, known also in different sources as Siegfried, in which guise he appears in Wagner's opera cycle *The Ring of the Nibelungs*. The curse of the Nibelungs for the theft of their treasure by the Aesir in order to pay Fafnir devolved on Sigurd, a member of the Volsungs, with its attendant legacy of treason and murder. Sigurd killed Fafnir with the sword Gram, forged for him by Regin the smith, and woke the Valkyrie BRUNHILDA from her charmed sleep, but betrayed her by marrying Gudrun as a result of drinking a magic draft of forgetfulness. Brunhilda in turn married Gudrun's brother Gunnar and plotted Sigurd's death in vengeance, thus fulfilling the Nibelungs' curse.

SIN

(Sumerian Nanna-Su'en), the Mesopotamian moon god, son of ENLIL and Ninlil, husband of Ningal and father to SHAMASH and ISHTAR. His principal cult was located in the city of Ur, where he was particularly venerated by the kings of the Ur III dynasty, and at Harran in south Turkey, especially under the Neo-Babylonian king Nabonidus (555-539 BC), who also took his cult worship to Teima in Arabia. His symbol is the crescent moon.

SISYPHUS

In Greek myth a mortal trickster, 'most crafty of men', who got the better of the Greek gods until confined to Hades, continuously rolling a rock up a hill but unable to stop it from rolling back down again. He was the son of Aeolus. Sisyphus' cattle were often stolen by Autolocus, so on the eve of the marriage of Autolocus' daughter Anticleira Sisyphus stopped this by attaching to the feet of the cattle lead tablets saying 'stolen by Autolocus'. That night Sisyphus found his way into Anticleira's bed and she conceived, bearing a son who was ODYSSEUS, as wily as Sisyphus himself.

Another story told how Sisyphus annoyed ZEUS by revealing to Asopus where Zeus had taken Asopus' daughter. Zeus' punishment was to send Thanatos (death) to Sisyphus but Sisyphus surprised Thanatos and chained him up. No mortal died until Zeus forced Sisyphus to free Thanatos, enabling him to kill Sisyphus. The wily Sisyphus arranged for his wife not to perform funerary rites, as a pretext for his return from Hades. Sisyphus eventually died of old age and received his punishment in Hades rolling his rock. A shrine to him was set up on the Acrocorinth near Corinth.

Below Sirens decorate this sixth century BC Greek dish; they were shown variously as nymphs or as birds with women's heads and they tempted sailors to death with their sweet songs. Only Odysseus managed to resist their enchantment by having himself tied to the mast.

Above and right   The sphinx was a mythical creature with the bust of a woman, the body of a dog, the tail of a serpent, the paws of a lion and a human voice. It was sent as a curse to Thebes by Hera and devoured those travelers who could not answer its riddle but was finally vanquished by Oedipus. In historical times the sphinx was regarded by the Egyptians as a sacred creature and here (above) lines the avenue leading to the Luxor temple and (right) decorates a Greek grave slab.

SOBEK

Egyptian crocodile god, with close associations with the monarch arising from the concept of instant destruction for any enemy. His mother was the creator goddess NEITH of Sais. In Upper Egypt the temple of Kombo, picturesquely perched on the bank of the Nile, was sacred to Sobek in its eastern sector; he was worshiped along with his wife HATHOR and their child KHONSU.

SOKAR

Egyptian hawk god worshiped in the Memphite necropolis. He amalgamated with the great creator god of Memphis to become 'Ptah-Sokar'. In Underworld scenes Sokar became the 'lord of the mysterious region' and his head emerged from the sand mound over which the sun god passed in a gesture of resurrection. His festival emphasized the resurrection of the god-king.

SULIS

A pre-Roman water deity associated with the natural hot springs rising out of the Mendips at Bath, Somerset, England. In Roman times her therapeutic strength was soon recognized and led to the development of the area into a large temple complex and bathing establishment. Her name was incorporated into the name of the new town, *Aquae Sulis*, and there is also a conflation with MINERVA to produce the deity Sulis-Minerva. Since 1727 many structural remains have been recovered from the area of the baths at Bath and also superb finds that include the famous bronze head from the goddess' cult statue and the MEDUSA Gorgon stone head from the temple pediment. Since the 1880s proper excavations have taken place, especially in the last 20 years when much epigraphic evidence of Sulis has emerged from the depths in the shape of lead curse tablets. The goddess is invoked to right all sorts of wrongs, theft of property and of affections, and rewards are promised to her if the miscreant is brought to light. Native Celtic and Roman elements come strongly together in the area to create an identifiably separate culture and it is noteworthy how many aspects of healing cults are located around or close to the Severn Estuary, e.g. NODENS.

Left Water flows over Roman masonry from the thermal spring in the great complex devoted to the goddess Sul Minerva at Bath, England.

TAMMUZ

Babylonian equivalent of the Syrian fertility god Atis, and the consort and brother of the earth and mother goddess ISHTAR. His annual death, resurrection and marriage indicate a fertility ritual connected with the agricultural cycle; an Akkadian fragment describes the ritual wailing of Ishtar for Tammuz and her descent into the Underworld.

TANTALUS

In Greek myth he was punished in Hades for some impiety. The different reasons for his punishment included stealing the gods' nectar to give to mortal friends; revealing the gods' secrets; serving up the flesh of his son Pelops to the gods; stealing ZEUS' guard dog on Crete. He was punished by being 'tantalized': hungry and thirsty, he was placed in front of a pool of water and fruit trees. When he tried to drink, the water receded and when he tried to eat, the wind blew the branches of the fruit trees away. Another version

had Tantalus sitting at a banquet, unable to eat for fear that the rock suspended over his head might fall on him.

Tantalus was a son of Zeus or a son of Troilus; he was the father of Pelops and his descendants included Thyestes and the house of ATREUS.

TARANIS

A Celtic thunder god who was equated with JUPITER. Like his classical counterpart, he was represented holding a thunderbolt (*fulmen*) and he also had a wheel set down beside him, an emblem of the solar nature of his cult. Despite his obvious importance, he is only referred to on a single inscription from Roman Britain, an altar dedicated at Chester (*Deva*) by a senior centurion of the Twentieth Legion.

He is represented as an otherwise unidentified god holding a crooked stick and shield with his wheel beside him on a well known pottery mold from Corbridge (*Corstopitum*). As a thunder god Taranis occurs widely with his wheel in Celtic Gaul and has affinities with similar deities in numerous other areas and times, e.g. THOR in the north and TESHUB in the Ancient Near East.

Far left In the classical world the temple was always built in the most commanding and prominent position. Here the temple of Poseidon rules the sea at Sounion.

Left Taranis, the Celtic god of thunder who was often also represented with a wheel, from a ritual silver cauldron found in a bog in Denmark.

TARPEIA

The daughter of the governor of the citadel in Rome. Tempted by the gold on the Sabines' bracelets and collars, she allowed their army to enter the fortress but was crushed to death by them. In one version Tarpeia had demanded, in return for favors, what the Sabines had on their arms. While this can be taken to mean their adornments, it might also imply their shields which crushed her to death. She was buried on the Capitoline Hill in Rome, giving her name to the Tarpeian Rock at its south-west corner.

TAWERET

Egyptian goddess who, despite being represented as a terrifying pregnant hippopotamus, was one of the most delightful and benign deities. She was the protectress of women in childbirth and dangerous enough to ward off hostile threats at that crucial period. From this personal role Taweret is translated to a comic deity as 'lady of the horizon' forming the constellation of the Hippopotamus as conceived by the Egyptians to exist in the northern sky.

TEFNUT

Egyptian goddess personifying the moisture inherent in the atmosphere. Created from the semen or spittle of ATUM together with her brother-consort SHU, Tefnut, as daughter of the sun god, became his 'Eye' and could take the form of a raging lioness.

TELEPHUS

In Greek myth the son of HERACLES and Auge and king of Mysia in Asia Minor. Several versions of his story exist; the most usual is that after his birth on Mount Parthenon he was abandoned at sea with his mother and their ship drifted to Mysia, where he was brought up at court. The tragedians, in works now lost, focus on the recognition of Telephus and Auge in a longer version of the story. Telephus was given Auge in marriage as a reward for helping to defend Mysia for King Teuthras, but Auge remained faithful to Heracles' memory and was unwilling to marry a mortal. She went into the marriage chamber carrying a sword, but a snake rose up between the two, preventing incest and murder and allowing her time to recognize her son.

Telephus was wounded by ACHILLES when the Greeks landed in Mysia on their way to fight at Troy. The Delphic oracle told him cryptically that the wounder would also heal him. Telephus helped the Greeks find their way to the Troad eight years later when they returned and, as his reward, Achilles agreed to heal him with the rust on his spear.

TESHUB

The characteristic god of Anatolia, as with Syria, is the weather god, depicted as driving in his chariot pulled by bulls. In the Hurrian pantheon this god is called Teshub, whose wife was Hebat. Teshub's father was Kumarbi, and the *Song of Ullikummi* tells of a conspiracy launched by Kumarbi against Teshub, who had usurped his place as king of the gods. Kumarbi recruits the sea in the contest, the child Ullikummi is born, and set on the shoulders of Upelluri in the sea, who attains enormous size. Teshub uses an ancient knife to combat Ullikummi's magic diorite stone, and renders him powerless. This myth has been compared to the Greek myth of Typhon; see also ADAD and BAAL.

TEUTATES

One of the most powerful of the Celtic deities in Gaul and one of the few singled out for special mention by the Roman writer Lucan, who also associates human sacrifice with the god. On several inscriptions, notably on a group of large silver plaques from Barkway, Hertfordshire, his name is associated with that of MARS. He is obviously equated in Britain with Mars as a war god.

THESEUS

In Greek myth the national hero of Athens. He was the son of Aethra by either Aegeus, king of Athens, or POSEIDON, who in some versions slept with Aethra on the same night that she slept with the childless Aegeus. Many parts of Theseus' tale were elaborated by the Greek tragedians and by the fifth century BC there was a strong revival of interest in him as ancestral king and founder of Athenian democracy. As a hero he was identified closely with HERACLES and his story is similar in some elements, especially the killing of enemies, but Theseus mainly killed brigands and robbers of travelers, whereas Heracles killed more exotic monsters. Theseus is said to have joined with Heracles and JASON in the expedition for the Golden Fleece and in the hunt for the Calydonian boar, but this warps the chronology, Theseus being too young to have been part of them. There is a possibility that Theseus was a historical figure but this cannot be proved.

Theseus was brought up at Troezen. Before his birth Aegeus had placed his own sword and sandals under a heavy stone for his son to take at his manhood. So when Theseus was strong enough he traveled to Athens and lifted the stone to take the sandals and sword. On his way there he encountered several enemies and slew them with ease. When he arrived at Athens his father recognized him only by the sword he had left under the stone, which Theseus used to cut his meat. MEDEA was at that time Aegeus' wife and had tried to poison Theseus in order to maintain her influence. She then set Theseus to kill a bull which Heracles had brought back from Crete and which was devastating Marathon. This Theseus did with ease; his next task was more difficult. The yearly tribute of seven girls and seven youths to the MINOTAUR was again due from Athens so Theseus went as part of the tribute to destroy the Minotaur. ARIADNE, Minos' daughter, fell in love with Theseus and helped him to retrace his steps through the labyrinth by a reel of thread. He took her back with him but then abandoned her on Naxos. He then caused his father Aegeus to jump off the cliff to his death because he had forgotten to change the black sails of his outward journey to white for a triumphant return.

As mythical king Theseus reorganized Attica as a confederacy of states, with Athens its capital, and began to set up a democracy. But he had to quell an Amazon invasion caused possibly by his abduction of the Amazon queen, HIPPOLYTA, to be his wife. With Peirithous, the Lapith king, he tried to abduct HELEN for himself and PERSEPHONE for Peirithous, from Hades; they were kept in Hades permanently until rescued by Heracles. His bones were brought back to Athens in the fifth century BC by the aristrocratic leader Cimon, and placed in Athens in the temple known as the Theseum.

Below left Theseus kills the Minotaur while Ariadne hovers anxiously in the background, on this badly damaged Greek red-figure vase.

Below right A muscular Theseus lifts the rock to reveal his father's sword. This was a test of manhood and was the first step in a heroic career that culminated in the killing of the Minotaur.

Above Thor sits in a boat with the giant who is trying to hoodwink him and fishes for the World Serpent with the head of an ox, on this fragment from a tenth century cross.

Right Silver amulet of the Viking period in the shape of Thor's hammer, presumably used as a charm to ward off injury in battle.

THOR

The god of the North about whom most tales and legends are told. He was one of the sons of ODIN and recognized especially as a weather god with huge strength. Of all the Norse and Viking gods he was the one with the closest parallels in the early religions of the ancient Near and Far East, in Anatolia and India. Thor was the great adventurer and traveler, often being involved with the Giants.

His weapon and emblem was his hammer, Mjolnir (or Mullicrusher). He had two other wonderful possesions, a strength-increasing belt and a pair of iron gauntlets that enabled him to wield his hammer.

Among his travels he visited Outgard and was hoodwinked by seemingly simple challenges into performing great feats. Challenged to empty a drinking horn that did seem a little long, he found he could hardly lower the level of the liquid in it – it ended in the sea and the resulting difference in sea level is now known as the foreshore. Goaded into endeavoring to lift a large gray cat off its four paws and only managing to lift one, he found it was really the World Serpent disguised and the world nearly fell apart. In a wrestling match against an old and withered crone he stood firm and only eventually dropped to one knee; the contest was against old age itself. Annoyed at the way he had been duped, Thor went fishing for the World Serpent using a fresh ox head as bait on his line. The bait was taken and Thor projected all his great strength to lift the Serpent's head up from the depths of the sea. When its head came above the boat's gunwale the giant with Thor, Hymir, was terrified and hacked Thor's fishing rod in two, letting the Serpent sink back into the sea.

A major myth tells of how Thor lost his famous hammer. He woke one day to find that it had been stolen by the Giants. The king of the Giants was only prepared to return it if the gods promised him FREYA, the goddess of love and beauty, for his wife. The gods knew that they would be powerless against the Giants if they attacked Asgard without Thor's hammer to defend them and could see no way out of the dilemma. Thor, in a rage at the terms, said that Freya must go and submit but HEIMDALL came up with a crafty solution. He suggested that Thor himself should go disguised as the bride, heavily veiled and wearing Freya's great and distinctive necklace, Brisingamen, around his neck to allay suspicion. Thor was reluctant to dress as a woman, but the entreaties of the gods and LOKI's offer to go along similarly dressed as a maid servant persuaded him.

The procession set out in a chariot drawn by goats and the giants prepared the reception. At the wedding feast early in the evening the 'bride' consumed a whole ox, eight salmon and all the delicacies put out for the ladies; it was all washed down with three tuns of mead. The Giant King was amazed at his 'bride's' appetite but cunning Loki told him that 'she' had not eaten for a week in happy anticipation of being married. At last the ceremony began and, in the traditional way, Thor's hammer was laid on the 'bride's' lap. Once more with Mjolnir his hammer in his hand, Thor leapt to his feet and immediately despatched the Giant King and those giants nearby. Thus he regained his hammer.

At the Ragnarok Thor was killed by Jormungand, the World Serpent.

THOTH

In Egyptian mythology the vizier or deputy of the sun god, with responsibility for scribal knowledge and science. His emblem was the moon and he could be represented as a baboon. The other way in which Thoth could be shown was either completely or with the head of the sacred ibis – the earliest and most stately portrayal of the god. The curved beak of the ibis suggested the crescent of the moon while the black and white feathering symbolized the waxing and waning of the moon. The association of the god Thoth with scribes permeated Egyptian society. It was Thoth who gave the knowledge of writing in the hieroglyphic script to the Egyptians, and so hieroglyphics were always thought to be charged with a magical force. Because Thoth was impartial and unsusceptible to bribes he was in charge of the scales weighing the hearts of the deceased persons in the Underworld to see if their crimes were too severe for them to enter the realm of OSIRIS. He declared those who passed the rigorous examination of their past life as 'True of Voice' or justified.

TYR

A Norse warrior god and the most cold bloodedly brave of them all. He was often identified with the Roman MARS. In the legends it was Tyr who was prepared to make the sacrifice of his hand in the jaws of the wolf FENRIR so that the gods could buy time in shackling him with the magic chain Gleipnir. At the Ragnarok Tyr died like ODIN, being swallowed by a wolf, Garm. The two gods have much in common and Tyr may have been an earlier chief god than Odin but was then displaced into his warrior status.

Below Thoth, the ibis-headed god, gives the Pharaoh the *ankh*, symbol of life, during the daily temple ritual.

ULYSSES see ODYSSEUS

URANUS

In Greek myth the son of GAIA (Earth) and also her husband. As the personification of Sky, Uranus was connected with the fertility of earth; he covered it and by it he had many children including CRONUS. But he hated his children and confined them to Tartarus (part of the Underworld) as soon as they were born. Gaia was sick of continual childbearing so she persuaded Cronus to castrate Uranus and dethrone him. The severed testicles, thrown into the sea, took root as an island; from the drops of blood sprang the race of Giants and from the foam round his limbs in the sea APHRODITE sprang. In a different version, told by Diodorus Siculus, Uranus was a king skilled in astronomy who, on his death, became identified with the sky itself.

UTANAPISH-TIM

(Sumerian Ziusudra), a Sumerian king and flood hero who appears in the Old Babylonian *Sumerian Flood Story* (sometimes called *The Eridu Genesis*) credited with saving mankind from destruction and rewarded with eternal life in the land of Dilmun. In a different Sumerian composition, *The Instructions of Shuruppak*, Ziusudra received practical advice on the art of living from his father Shuruppak, in the form of short proverbial sayings.

In the *Babyloniaca* of Berrossus his name survives as Xisouthros in the Greek version of the old Mesopotamian Flood story. Utanapishtim is his counterpart in the Epic of GILGAMESH; see also ATRA-HASIS.

Far left Hades, Greek god of the Underworld, entertains the fair Persephone on this fifth century BC Greek vase. He had stolen her from earth and, while incarcerated in his realm, she made the mistake of eating seven pomegranate seeds and was thus condemned to spend part of every year with him.

Left Ulysses, the Greek Odysseus, and his companions drive a stake into the eye of the Cyclops Polyphemus in their efforts to escape his clutches during Ulysses's protracted return journey from the Trojan War.

VANIR

In Norse mythology a race of gods who seem to have preceded the AESIR. At first there was war between the two but peace was made by both sides ritually spitting into the magic cauldron of the giants. FREY and FREYA came originally from the Vanir; Frigg and Frigga were the Aesir equivalents.

VENUS

The Roman goddess of love, associated from the second century BC with APHRODITE. Very little is known of the worship of Venus but her cult began in pre-Roman Italy, where she was the deity of gardens and vegetation. This cult was widespread, with festivals during April as a later addition.

Venus was known as the daughter of JUPITER and Dione, but the better-known story is that she was born from the foam of the sea and wafted by the wind to Cyprus. Venus' son, CUPID, acted on her instructions to fire individuals such as PSYCHE with love by the touch of his arrow. She also had a magic girdle which inspired love. Venus was the victim of her own schemes when she wounded herself with one of Cupid's arrows; the first man she saw was ADONIS, for whom she developed an instant passion. Anxious not to lose him, she tried but failed to persuade him to stop hunting, and he was killed by a boar.

The name Venus means 'beauty' or 'charm' and it is for this quality that she was famed. The Emperor Augustus' family, the Julians, claimed to be descended from AENEAS, son of Venus by Anchises.

Far left The Venus de Milo, marble statue from the second century BC, is one of the most loved and famous images of the Roman goddess of love.

Left This cross at Gosforth, Cumbria, northern England, is carved with Viking myths, including the destruction of the Vanir and Aesir at Ragnarok, set in a Christian context.

Below left Venus rides on gooseback across the interior of a fifth century BC kylix or cup.

Below right Exquisite silver and gilt Venus rising from the waves on her conch shell, a detail from the fourth century AD Projecta Casket, which represents a blend of pagan and Christian themes.

Right The round temple of Vesta, guardian goddess of Rome, in the Forum, where the sacred fire burned that kept Rome safe from her enemies.

Right The chastely draped figure of a Vestal Virgin, who tended the sacred fire, stands in the House of the Vestals in the Forum.

VESTA

One of the ten great Roman dieties and identified with the Greek Hestia, goddess of the hearth. Vesta was the guardian of Rome and while her sacred fire burned, Rome remained safe. The fire was allowed to go out on the first day of March (New Year's Day) and was relit; if it went out at any other time there were heavy penalties. The fire was tended by four Vestal Virgins, taken originally from patrician families, who served for 30 years each and then returned to their home lives. The penalty for being unchaste was burial alive in an underground chamber. The festival of Vesta, the Vestalia, was celebrated on 9 June each year. This was a rest day for asses from the mills and they were decked with violets and strings of loaves; the ass was Vesta's sacred animal and symbol, because – as a late story tells – an ass had protected Vesta from PRIAPUS' amorous advances. During the week of the Vestalia, matrons brought offerings to the temple of Vesta where they were kept in the storehouse. After this the temple was cleaned and set up as normal once more.

VOLSUNGS

In Norse mythology a family of heroes descended from the legendary king Volsung. Sigmund was his son and SIGURD his grandson. Sigmund was one of the chosen of ODIN, who gave him a sword; when the time came for his death, Odin again appeared and shattered the blade in battle so that Sigmund was killed.

VULCAN

The Roman smith god, identified with the Greek HEPHAESTUS. He was traditionally introduced to Rome by either ROMULUS or Titus Tatius. There were no specific legends concerning Vulcan but he played an important part in the success of various heroes by providing invincible armor for them. In Virgil's *Aeneid*, Vulcan made a superb suit of armor for AENEAS at VENUS' request. He made a shield (called the Aegis) and thunderbolts for JUPITER and in return received VENUS as his wife. This makes for a surprising couple, given Venus' famed beauty and the fact that Vulcan was born lame: his mother, JUNO, was so ashamed of him that she threw him out of heaven.

At the Vulcanalia, or Festival of Vulcan, little fish and other small animals were thrown into fires. These offerings represented human lives and were made in order to spare humans from death.

Above Carved cart from a Norwegian ship-burial of the ninth century AD, showing the warrior Gunnar in the snakepit into which he was cast by Sigurd the Volsung.

Below left The Roman smith god Vulcan forges arrows for Cupid on a sixteenth century Italian earthenware dish.

Below right Roman bronze of Vulcan, possibly carrying the thunderbolts he forged for Jupiter.

187

WAYLAND

In northern legend a smith god. Gifted in his craft of working all metals, he was once a prince, one of three brothers each of whom married a swan maiden. One night when he was alone in his workshop he was captured by the evil king Nidud, Lord of the Niars. The king accused Wayland of stealing his gold and himself proceeded to take Wayland's sword and give one of his magic gold rings to his daughter, Bodvild. Nidud's queen did not like the look of Wayland and suggested that the sinews in his legs be cut to make him lame. He was then marooned on a tiny island with a work-shop close to the mainland, which only the king was allowed to visit.

Wayland worked day and night, always hanker-ing for the return of his sword and ring and plot-ting his revenge. One day the king's two young sons came secretly to the island and demanded Wayland's keys to his chest so that they could see all the treasures in it. Wayland persuaded them to tell no one of their visit and return the next day, when he would give them all the treasure for themselves. They duly returned and he began his revenge. First he cut off their heads and hid the bodies in a rubbish heap. Their skulls he mounted in silver as a gift to their father Nidud; he made their eyes into precious stones for their mother and their teeth he worked into two breast ornaments for their sister Bodvild. She was curious to see the smith at work and so she broke the ring that she wore, stolen in the first place from Wayland, and went to him secretly to repair it. While he worked he plied her with beer until she was helpless, then he raped her. His revenge was then complete on the family of Nidud and he fled the island, flying away on a pair of wings he had made.

Wayland's legend has much in common with that of the Greek smith god HEPHAESTUS and also the master craftsman DAEDALUS. His name appears quite widely in place names such as the Neolithic long barrow on the Berkshire Downs, Wayland's Smithy. He is also connected with Christian legend, being depicted on one of the walrus ivory front panels of the Northumbrian seventh-century Franks Casket. Here he is shown with the head of one of the king's sons in his tongs and also in company with birds, a reference either to the swan maidens or to his flight.

WEPWAWET

Ancient Egyptian jackal deity of Upper Egypt parti-cularly in the regions of Abydos and Assint. The name Wepwawet means 'opener of the ways' which could be interpreted as a promulgator of royal conquests abroad. In a funerary context the adze of Wepwawet was one of the implements used to touch the royal mummy in the ceremony of vivication known as 'opening the mouth'. He also guided the deceased on a good path through the perils of the Underworld.

Far left Wepwawet, the Egyptian jackal-headed god, stands on the far right of this group of underworld deities attending on Osiris, Judge of the Dead.

Below Wayland the Smith labors in his forge while his brother Egil fights the Niars, a detail from the Anglo-Saxon Franks casket.

ZEUS

The supreme Greek god and ruler of all the other gods as well as of men. He was the son of CRONUS and, with his brothers POSEIDON and HADES, siezed power from Cronus. Zeus took control originally of just the sky, but by the time of the Homeric epics, he was all-powerful. He manifested his power in the shape of storms with thunder and lightning, but was primarily concerned with justice. Thus murders were avenged in his name, oaths kept and hospitality upheld, and punishments dealt out to those who failed to deal justly. In the *Iliad* Zeus is shown with two jars from which he dispenses good and evil, usually in a mixture but sometimes just one or other. Thus Zeus controls the fates of men but he himself is subject to the FATES, who are Zeus' own offspring and so can be seen as an aspect of him, acting as a sort of conscience.

Zeus features in the Homeric poems in particular, but there are many different stories concerning his birth and life. When he was born he was said to have been put in a cave on Mount Dicte or Mount Ida on Crete and suckled by a nymph. When he had grown up, he made his father Cronus spew up the children he had swallowed and with his brothers displaced Cronus. The expulsion of the Titans from Heaven completed their victory. It was at this point that Zeus took power over the sky and the universe, dwelling on Mount Olympus. But the Giants and Typhon provided further obstacles to his power. When PROMETHEUS had created men from clay, Zeus refused to give them fire so Prometheus stole fire from Olympus. Zeus punished Prometheus and then the whole of mankind by sending a flood to wipe them all out.

Thus Zeus intervened in all aspects of human and divine life. He assisted in the labors of HERACLES and intervened in the frequent quarrels between APOLLO and HERACLES over the tripod of Delphi. In all things justice was done, but Zeus' justice can seem rather harsh and extreme.

Zeus' wife HERA was not alone in bearing his children, and although he was not literally the father of all gods, he was connected with most of the branches of demigods and heroes throughout Greek mythology. Not surprisingly, his many affairs caused Hera some irritation, but Zeus was unaffected. His first wife had been Metis (Prudence), who was mother of ATHENA by Zeus; it was predicted that after bearing a daughter she would have a son who would dethrone his father. So Zeus swallowed Metis and Athena was born, fully armed, from his head. To avoid the dangerous second child, Zeus then married Themis, and their children included Dike (Justice), Eunomia (Discipline), Eirene (Peace) and the Horae

(Seasons). He was also father of the FATES, hence the different aspects of Zeus are sprung from and part of him.

APHRODITE was Zeus' daughter by Dione; other important offspring included Apollo and ARTEMIS. His marriage to Hera may have taken place at this point or earlier, and he had three children by her. Of Zeus' frequent affairs with mortals, many were carried out with Zeus in the shape of a particular animal. EUROPA was taken by a bull which was Zeus; DANAE was made pregnant by Zeus when he appeared through a tiny chink in the wall of her prison as a shower of gold; and GANYMEDE was carried off by an eagle, again Zeus. In antiquity these affairs were viewed with a mixture of disapproval and philosophical understanding. Some saw them as part of the destiny of creation by which, for example, Heracles was born of Zeus to rid the earth of monsters.

Far left Roman tomb relief showing Zeus with his daughter Artemis.

Below The sacred cave at the heart of Olympia, a major Greek sanctuary sacred to Zeus and his consort Hera.

Bottom Roman mosaic from Lullingstone villa, Kent, England, showing Zeus in one of his many disguises carrying off Europa.

ACKNOWLEDGMENTS

The publisher would like to thank Cathy Shilling, the designer, Maria Costantino, the picture researcher, and Jessica Orebi Gann, the editor. Thanks are also due to Princeton University Press for permission to use the material from Joseph Campbell's *The Hero With a Thousand Faces*.

All photographs supplied courtesy of **CM Dixon, Photo Resources,** Kingston, Kent, except for the following:

Bison Picture Library pages 6, 12, 43, 58, 97, 101 top, 116, 118, 176

Courtesy, The Trustees of the British Museum pages 39 below, 73 below, 152

Archiv Gerstenberg pages 7, 14, 24, 30 below, 34, 64, 80 top, 90, 95, 96 below, 99 top, 134, 150, 155, 157 below, 160, 162, 185 right

Fred Gettings page 191 top

The Metropolitan Museum of Art, pages 42, 76, 79 top, 100 below, 174 below

Munich Antikensammlung page 72

Musée du Louvre, Paris/Photo RMN pages 154 left, 159 top

National Archeological Museum, Athens pages 8 top, 40, 127 top, 129, 131 left

National Museum, Copenhagen page 15 below

National Museum, Naples page 21

Römermuseum, Augst, Switzerland page 16

Römer-Pelizaeus Museum, Hildesheim page 128

Mick Sharp/LPR Adkins page 158 below/Dave Longley pages 37 top, 60, 175

The Warburg Institute, University of London page 70, 191 below